OPPORTUNITIES IN
AIRLINE CAREERS

Adrian A. Paradis

Foreword by
Robert H. Wood
Founding Editor, *Aviation Daily*

 VGM Career Horizons
A Division of National Textbook Company
4255 West Touhy Avenue
Lincolnwood, Illinois 60646-1975 U.S.A.

Cover photo credits

Front Cover: upper left and lower right,
United Airlines; upper right, Delta Airlines;
lower left, Charles Gerity.

Back Cover: upper and lower left, Delta
Airlines; upper right, Air France; lower right,
Scandinavian Airlines System.

1988 Printing

Copyright © 1987 by National Textbook Company
4255 West Touhy Avenue
Lincolnwood (Chicago), Illinois 60646-1975 U.S.A.
All rights reserved. No part of this book may
be reproduced, stored in a retrieval system, or
transmitted in any form or by any means, electronic,
mechanical, photocopying, recording or otherwise,
without the prior permission of National Textbook Company.
Manufactured in the United States of America.
Library of Congress Catalog Number: 86-62037

8 9 0 BC 9 8 7 6 5 4 3 2

ABOUT THE AUTHOR

Adrian A. Paradis was born in Brooklyn, New York, and graduated from Dartmouth College and Columbia University's School of Library Service. As a writer, businessman, vocational specialist, and researcher, he has published widely with more than fifty titles to his credit. He has covered subjects that range from banking to biographies; from public relations to religion; from vocational guidance to reference works; and from economics to law.

Mr. Paradis spent over twenty years as an officer of a major airline handling corporate matters, economic analysis, stockholder relations, corporate philanthropic contributions, and security and general administrative responsibilities. He and his wife Grace live in Sugar Hill, New Hampshire, where he serves as editor of Phoenix Publishing, a small firm which specializes in regional trade books and New England town histories.

FOREWORD

Aviation is still one of our most glamorous industries. As it continues to expand it should offer you exciting job opportunities, security, and a fascinating lifestyle during your working hours. Best of all, it has a tradition of seeking and trying new ways to serve the public better, constantly asking itself, "How can we improve everything we do?" This means there will be unexpected opportunities for those who use their skills and imagination to further the progress and growth of this great business.

Here, in one volume, you can learn about every part of the airline business, from a beginning job as a clerk in a mail room, to reservations agent, passenger service representative, airplane cleaner, mechanic, operations manager, aircraft controller, to the position of a pilot in charge of a huge airliner carrying as many as four hundred passengers.

Adrian Paradis tells you about so many jobs that you will readily see why this is truly a business which offers something for everyone. Let Mr. Paradis give you a guided tour of an airline administrative department in a Chicago skyscraper. Go with him as he conducts a tour of the airport and operations offices of a typical airline. Watch how flight attendants handle their jobs, and stand in the cockpit of a jet airplane to see how the crew skillfully takes off from California, then lands at Kennedy Airport in New York City. There are many insights here to a variety of occupations. Thus, the book is an exciting introduction to a fascinating business which you will want to investigate further. You can do this by reading some of the books Mr. Paradis mentions in the Suggested Readings to further familiarize yourself with those jobs which intrigue you.

As one who has spent many years working for an airline and an aircraft manufacturer, as well as editing several aviation publications, I have seen every angle of the business. I recommend that you investigate aviation for yourself and consider joining the many thousands of men and women who, day in and day out, keep the airplanes of this essential transportation industry flying both here and elsewhere around the world.

Robert H. Wood
Founder and formerly Editor of *Aviation Daily,* American Aviation Publications, and *Aviation Week Magazine*

CONTENTS

accounting. Payroll. Insurance. Tax administration. Budget.

Flight officers train for many years before qualifying as pilots on passenger-carrying airline. Photo: United Airlines.

CHAPTER 1

INTRODUCTION

GETTING THE MAIL THROUGH

It was early on the morning of May 15, 1918, when a fair-sized crowd gathered at one end of a small polo field between the Potomac River and the Tidal Basin in Washington. Although World War I was raging in France, President Wilson, members of his cabinet, and other dignitaries took time out from their busy day to watch the inauguration of air-mail service between the nation's capital and New York. An airplane was to fly the mail from Washington to Philadelphia where a waiting plane would take it on to New York. A similar service would operate southbound.

The brief ceremony culminated in the stowing of four sacks of mail in the little plane. Then Lieutenant George L. Boyle climbed aboard and the propeller swung around but the engine failed to catch. Again and again the prop was rotated but nothing happened. The onlookers' patience was nearly exhausted when a mechanic who was peering into the gas tanks discovered that someone had forgotten to fill them. There was a scurry to find fuel. At last it was poured into the plane and then, with a brave wave to the crowd, the pilot started the engine and took off.

As the spectators returned to their waiting cars, Lieutenant Boyle climbed out of sight, but soon lost his way and crash-landed on a farm in southeastern Maryland, twenty-five miles from Washington. Meanwhile, Lieutenant Torrey H. Webb piloted mail from New York to Philadelphia, where Lieutenant James C. Edgerton picked up the relay. The gray canvas bags reached the capital without delay three hours and twenty minutes after leaving Long Island's old Belmont race track which then served as New York City's airport. Thus the nation's first regularly scheduled air mail took to the skies.

FROM NOVELTY TO BENEFITS

When these historic flights were made airplanes were still a novelty to the public. Some six years before, in 1913, the first scheduled passenger service began between St. Petersburg and Tampa, Florida; but it lasted less than five months. Again in 1919 two new companies started operating, one between New York City and Atlantic City and the other from Florida to Havana, Cuba, and the Bahamas. During the succeeding years a few other companies were organized, and all had one thing in common: they used flying boats, not planes as they are known to us today, because at that time there were few adequate or safe airports. In 1923 the only regularly scheduled U.S. passenger airline closed down, but overseas in Europe thousands of people were flying a network of airline routes every day.

World War I had taught the Europeans what the airplane could do and how it might save travelers time and money. Americans, on the other hand, looked upon the tiny planes as a novelty, something to read about in fictional stories or in the newspapers if there was a crash. The railroad was still considered the only way to travel.

In 1925, all this changed. Congress passed the Kelly Act which authorized the Post Office Department to award twelve Civil Air Mail routes to carry the mail coast to coast as well as between principal cities. Almost immediately more than five thousand inquiries flooded the Post Office Department, as would-be airline operators eagerly sought information about how they might bid for the dozen routes. Their enthusiasm was further bolstered when President Coolidge signed the Air Commerce Act on May 20, 1926, creating the Aeronautics Branch in the Department of Commerce. Now the Secretary of Commerce could license pilots, issue airworthiness certificates for airplanes, establish a system of federal airways, and install and operate navigation aids. Aviation had finally become an established form of transportation in the United States.

Most of the small companies that hauled the air mail had neither interest nor capacity for carrying passengers. Occasionally a courageous individual might appear at an airport, request passage, and buy a ticket only to be cramped into the forward part of the plane and forced to sit on mail sacks. One honeymooning couple insisted on riding a mail flight and was charged a thousand dollars for a five hundred mile trip! An exception was Colonial Air Transport (a predecessor of American Airlines) which carried over four thousand passengers between New York and Boston during the first few months it started handling air mail. The company inaugurated its first night flights in 1927, about the same time Robertson Aircraft Corporation started service between Chicago and St. Louis.

NONSTOP TO PARIS

One of the pilots was a young man nicknamed "Slim" because of his slight build. Charles A. (Slim) Lindbergh frequently found flying conditions on Robertson's CAM-2 flight anything but pleasant or safe. On one occasion he was flying through light snow at night, unable to find a suitable landing place. His main tank went dry and nineteen minutes later the reserve needle showed empty while the plane was still at 14,000 feet. As the plane rolled over, "Slim" left it head first. He pulled the ripcord on his parachute, floated down slowly, and landed on a barbed-wire fence. The next morning he found the wrecked craft nearby. The mail bags were still intact and he delivered them to their destination in another plane.

In spite of the hazards the job seemed too tame for this young man. In 1927 Lindbergh realized a long-time dream when he became the first person to fly the Atlantic nonstop from New York to Paris.

Lindbergh's flight turned the thoughts of millions of Americans toward the skies and toward New York's then booming stock market, as well. Aviation stocks played an important role in the Wall Street frenzy which sent most stock prices zooming upward between 1926

and 1929. Bankers put together large aviation holding companies*
consisting of airlines, airplane manufacturing companies, airports,
and other aviation-related activities. They then sold stock to the gul-
lible public and with their friends made millions of dollars. Between
March 1928 and the end of 1929 sales of new aviation securities to-
taled $300,000,000 and increased in value to over $1,000,000,000.
The public was so eager to invest in aviation stocks that many people
bought stock in a company called Seaboard Airline. When they received their stock certificates and saw the engraving of a steam engine, they discovered they owned shares of an East Coast railroad,
rather than an airline!

THE '30s AND THE CIVIL AERONAUTICS ACT

Although the stock market crash of October 1929 squeezed most
of the value out of airline securities as it did most other stocks, it did
not ground the airplanes. The following year Postmaster Walter
Brown circumvented a new law Congress had passed to help the
struggling air transport companies. At a so-called "Spoils Confer-
ence" he saw to it that the large financial interests that were tied into
the holding companies received the best new routes and profitable
subsidies. Three new transcontinental routes were formed and others authorized, laying the foundation for much of the nation's present airline network. Despite the Depression (which started about the
time Postmaster Brown and the so-called "Spoilers" divided up the
airline map), the airlines continued to grow. In fact, some of their
competitive practices created problems for the public and themselves, making it evident that they had to be regulated by the federal
government just as the Interstate Commerce Commission watched
over the railroads. By the time the Civil Aeronautics Act became law
in 1938 it was accepted gracefully by the industry.

---

*A holding company retains ownership of other corporations and may pro-
vide overall direction and management to the subsidiary companies whose
stock it owns.

THE EFFECTS OF WORLD WAR II

Aviation gained further impetus during World War II as the airplane played a leading role in winning the war and making the nation more conscious of what it could do. As a result, in the year following the return of peace, twelve million Americans jammed in front of airline ticket counters eager to travel. Flying was the only way they wanted to go. Each year thereafter saw the number of passengers increase as the old twenty-one-passenger DC-3s were replaced by fifty-passenger DC-4s, and they, in turn, by larger DC-6s, DC-7s, and Lockheed Constellations. Then in 1958, the first Boeing 707 jet rose from the runway with a full load of passengers and freight, signaling the start of the jet age.

Jets not only made it possible to span the continent in some five hours, but for the first time hundreds of people could fly together in huge wide-body planes. Movies and gourmet meals brought new luxuries to those who could afford to sit up front in first class. At the same time, by dropping these frills and crowding more seats into the rear section of the cabin, "coach" travel, with its lower fares, enabled more Americans to fly who previously could never have purchased a ticket.

THE AIRLINE DEREGULATION ACT OF 1978

The Airline Deregulation Act of 1978 relaxed many provisions of the 1938 Civil Aeronautics Act and even provided for the dismantling of the Civil Aeronautics Board by January 1, 1985. This law made it possible for new and existing airlines to operate wherever they chose to fly. Competition was once again encouraged and rates started to drop at a time when costs were rising due to inflation and the cost of fuel. Nevertheless, more and more Americans were crowding the airports, thousands of them first-time flyers.

Passenger service representatives greet passengers and assure that ticketing and luggage check-in are handled efficiently. Photo: Scandinavian Airlines Systems.

IN 1986, 330,000 EMPLOYEES AND 365 MILLION PASSENGERS A YEAR

By 1986 air transportation had become one of the nation's most essential as well as largest industries. To realize just how big it is, consider that in 1986 some 330,000 employees were working for the nation's 92 commercial passenger and cargo air carriers, and 160 regional commuter airlines. These companies were transporting over 365 million passengers annually, accounting for most of the passenger travel between cities and almost all of the travel between the United States and cities overseas. Each day an average of over 14,500 flights took off from some 700 airports, offering speedy and reliable service to passengers while underneath the cabins the cargo compartments were crammed with mail, freight, and baggage.

As for aviation's future, during the 1985-1997 time period the FAA estimates that the industry will grow at a rate of about 5 percent each year. Continued growth spells continual new job opportunities —and employment security as well.

The cockpit crew meets before each flight to review the flight plan and discuss weather and other flight conditions. Photo: American Airlines.

CHAPTER 2

AIR TRANSPORTATION TODAY

In the crowded flight dispatch office three men were conferring about the weather and the projected flight plan. It was four o'clock Friday afternoon, just one hour before American Aviation Airlines Flight Number 5 was scheduled to take off from New York to Los Angeles. Jangling telephone bells and clattering teletype machines made conversation difficult. Several men and women came in, dropped their flight bags, and consulted maps hanging on the walls, while others picked up luggage and hurried out toward the airplanes they would be flying. The uniformed flight captain bent his head over the weather map spread out before him in the flight room. The meteorologist and flight dispatcher stood shaking their heads.

"Heavy turbulence over Missouri and Kansas," the meteorologist muttered, pointing with her pencil to the area around St. Louis.

"That means he better take the northern routing," the dispatcher said, and looking at the captain added, "You'll need every gallon to buck those winds and still make Los Angeles with enough reserve."

"Done it before," the captain said cheerfully without looking up. "Doubt I'll have any trouble getting into L.A.—perfect weather out there. Now, let's complete our flight plan."

Meanwhile, two miles away in a low white building, an assistant chef was squeezing whipped cream on top of two-hundred and ninety dishes of chocolate mousse. Within a half hour all the meals (fruit cup, fish or steak, potatoes, green beans, salad, rolls, butter, dessert, plus dishes, silverware, and napkins) would be loaded in a special catering truck and sped across the airport to be loaded via the rear cabin door onto Flight No. 5.

At Gate 19 on the B Concourse of the airport, the passenger service agent arrived. She put her cash and ticket stock in the counter drawer, and fixed the departure sign to read: "Flight 5—5:00 Departure for Los Angeles." Soon the first of the expected 280 passengers would be milling around the counter waiting to be checked in. Within a half hour two additional agents would be on hand to assist until departure time.

At the edge of the airport, in front of the company's hangar, a towering airplane, a Boeing 747, was being checked by mechanics. A tank truck was loading kerosene into the wing tanks while within the cabin a dozen men and women were vacuuming, distributing earphones packaged in cellophane, and polishing the windows. The airplane had arrived from Chicago only forty-five minutes earlier and had to be made ready for its five o'clock departure to Los Angeles.

On the fourteenth floor of a sky-scraper a thousand miles away, a group of men and women was studying a large blackboard which extended across one end of the room. The other walls displayed charts, graphs, maps and four clocks—showing Eastern, Central, Mountain, and Pacific time, respectively. All this information enabled those who worked here to keep track of every company aircraft, whether in the air or on the ground. If an airplane were late and might not be available for its next scheduled trip, or if it had to be taken out of service for emergency repairs or any other unexpected development, the people on duty in the operations room would decide how to cope with the problem: whether to substitute another plane, cancel the next flight, or take other action. Thanks to the company's extensive communications system, these operations specialists had their fingers on the pulse of the airline every minute of every day and were ready to make difficult decisions whenever required. Now, however, a glance at the charts told the chief supervisor that the aircraft for Flight No. 5 was being serviced and that the plane would be towed to its gate within fifteen minutes for an on-time departure.

Around five o'clock is one of the busiest times at any airport. Most business people want to depart at about that time and an airline will schedule as many flights as possible at rush hour because all seats will usually be filled. The station manager decided to take a brief tour of the loading gates.

The manager walked briskly down the corridor and paused at each departure lounge where customers were either waiting to board or were entering the airplane cabin. If he saw an unusually long line waiting to check in, he stopped to see why. On the other hand, if all appeared to be going well, he gave a word of commendation to the agents before passing on. Then, having satisfied himself that all was well, he hurried down to the ground floor and walked past the air-craft, each waiting for its appointed departure time. His eye was again alert to every detail, making sure that fleet service personnel were on hand, noting whether or not the airplanes were spotlessly clean, and whether the baggage and freight were being stowed prop-erly and carefully into the belly compartments. By the time he re-turned to his office it was five o'clock. A moment later Flight No. 5 passed his window en route to runway number 2–A where it waited for clearance.

Although the four-and-a-half hour trip of Flight No. 5 is the re-sponsibility of Air Traffic Control once the plane is airborne, radio operators in the company's several flight dispatch offices are on duty ready to be in touch with the crew if necessary throughout the entire flight as the flight attendants serve beverages and meals, show mov-ies, and look after the passengers' needs. Only after the airplane has landed, the passengers have safely left the plane, the freight, mail, and baggage have been unloaded, and the captain has turned in the written flight report, will Flight No. 5 be finished and forgotten—until tomorrow when the whole process will be repeated.

Flight No. 5, as you know, is just one of about 14,500 flights oper-ated each day by our nation's airlines. The planning and organiza-tion needed in every company to ensure that each of its flights oper-ates on time, safely, and to the passengers' comfort and pleasure is a big order. It's no wonder that aviation has become such a large indus-try and employs so many men and women.

AN INDUSTRY OF MANY VARIED CAREERS

Employees have made the air transportation industry work and grow—they are its most important asset. Highly specialized career opportunities range from those requiring a college degree such as engineering, accounting, and law to piloting which requires many years of intensive training and experience. Custodians, mail clerks, and receptionists can also find employment opportunities within the industry. In fact, there are innumerable positions which call for a variety of educational backgrounds, skills, and personal characteristics.

Generally, a high school diploma is a minimum requirement in order to apply for employment with an airline. This is just the beginning, however, because most workers are given some on-the-job training regardless of their previous education. Thus, even though you may have special training as a flight attendant, ticket agent, or teletypist, the airline may schedule you to take its own training courses. Prior training gives you some advantage, but it is wise to check with those airlines where you hope to find work and learn what pre-employment training, if any, is required.

Very few industries are as conscious of the importance of training and retraining. From time to time airlines purchase new aircraft; update methods of handling reservations and ticketing; and install new accounting, baggage handling, and communications equipment, all of which require retraining employees in methods and techniques. These training programs also create added opportunities for advancement to positions on the airlines' various training staffs.

Because so many jobs involve direct contact with the public, in sales and reservations, checking in passengers at the terminal, or serving them in flight, many positions call for individuals who can write and speak correctly, are neat and presentable, courteous, and truly interested in being of service and help to customers. If you enjoy dealing with the public (and can tolerate occasional unwarranted abuse), many interesting opportunities await you. On the other hand, if you are an individual who is happiest working by yourself without having constant contact with others, there are also numerous other kinds of job openings from which to choose, which can provide satisfying and rewarding careers as well.

SALARIES AND WORKING CONDITIONS

As in any industry, the larger the company the greater the opportunities for better-paying jobs and advancement. The small commuter airline which operates a dozen planes and carries a couple hundred passengers a day cannot afford to pay the salaries of a major carrier which has more than 30,000 employees and well over a hundred offices and operations centers. There are advantages to working for a small airline, though. There is usually a high degree of employee loyalty to the company and to each other, and there is a chance to observe what makes an airline tick and learn several jobs. This invaluable experience can often enable an employee to move on to a larger company and enter a better-paying and more specialized position. As long as you remain in the same airline you will find that most promotions are made within the company if it is possible to fill a vacancy with a qualified worker.

Working conditions are also of concern, especially since the airline industry works "round-the-clock" and shift work is necessary for many jobs. Large numbers of employees must work evenings or all night, but higher wages are usually paid for afternoon and night shifts. One of the most common causes of job turnover is unhappiness with shift work, but there is no way to eliminate it. Most office workers enjoy comfortable working conditions but those who service the airplanes or have other outdoor assignments must contend with weather extremes. Most airline employees are not permitted to smoke while on the job if they are dealing with the public or working in or around aircraft where there is danger of fire.

Employees who are normally seen by the passengers or public usually wear uniforms. Cleaners, kitchen and cafeteria workers, and mechanics, who usually work behind the scenes, also wear uniforms while on the job. As a rule employees are required to purchase their own uniforms, but it should be pointed out that this eliminates the need to use personal clothing for working hours.

Many airlines provide a generous package of benefits to employees. Paid vacations, sick leave, holidays, employee suggestion systems with cash awards, credit unions, and free or reduced costs for air travel for employees and members of their families, top the list. Employees are often eligible for substantial discounts for travel on most United States and international airlines as well as for special discounts at holiday resort hotels. During the mid-1980s the Air Transport Association of America estimated that the average annual salary (including fringe benefits) of airline employees was about $42,500 or almost at the top for all American industry.

AIRLINE JOBS ARE WIDELY SCATTERED

Airline employment is concentrated in major metropolitan areas like Chicago, Los Angeles, Miami, New York, San Francisco, and Washington, D.C., where traffic is heaviest. Nevertheless there are excellent job opportunities in other cities including Atlanta, Boston, Dallas/Fort Worth, Denver, Detroit, Kansas City, Philadelphia, and Seattle, to name but a few. Tulsa, Oklahoma, is a good job center because American Airlines operates its maintenance and overhaul base there. In many coastal cities there are additional openings because foreign airlines terminate their flights and employ Americans as well as others to handle air freight and passenger business, as well as to service aircraft.

The fact that there are so many different types of air carriers increases the variety of job opportunities within this industry. Most people are familiar with the scheduled airlines which actually range in size from those with very few employees and two or three stations to the giants of the industry employing more than 30,000 employees at well over 100 locations. The larger the airline the greater the job opportunity—and also the competition for those jobs. Not only do large airlines like American, Eastern, Northwest, TWA, and United fly transcontinental routes, but a number of them fly overseas to Alaska, Hawaii, the Caribbean, and other continents as well.

Many smaller companies fly within various regions of the United States. They provide frequent service to smaller cities and connect them with the large traffic centers. At the same time helicopters offer service from the centers of some cities to the airports at the outskirts. Yet another group of companies flies light aircraft over short routes to connect with local as well as transcontinental service. With the phenomenal growth of air freight there are several air cargo lines which haul tremendous amounts of freight, as well as supplemental air carriers which carry passengers and cargo on unscheduled charter flights. Nor should we overlook the "Indirect Air Carriers," a term for specialized operations which include air ambulance service, air taxis, and charter services. All of these provide essential services which the country needs, as well as providing a multitude of job opportunities.

OPPORTUNITY AT AIRPORTS

Airports are important sources of employment too. There are approximately 16,000 airports in the United States and they vary from a cleared grassy strip of level land to an elaborate complex of hundreds of acres of ground, miles of runways and roads, numerous buildings and parking lots. Some airports employ thousands of men and women, not to mention regular airline crews who are stationed at the airports.

Several thousand American airports offer at least a minimum of service during the daytime. The services they provide may be merely selling aviation fuel and soft drinks at a tiny field to an occasional visiting plane, or they may be what you find in a major metropolitan airport complex, which caters to thousands of passengers and hundreds of daily flights operated by scheduled airlines and the owners of general aviation aircraft.

An airport may be owned by a single operator who does all of the work with or without assistants, or by an urban, regional, or interstate governmental authority. As you will see later in the book, airports are almost a separate business requiring workers with a variety of special skills. Like the airplanes they serve, airports have a fascination of their own and offer many unusual and challenging career opportunities.

It is hard to realize that this huge industry has experienced most of its real growth since World War II. It is a young business, and one which attracts youth. Most employees are proud to be associated with aviation, and are loyal and enthusiastic about their companies.

This is further demonstrated by the fact that turnover within the airlines has amounted to about 1 percent a month compared to 4 percent for American industry as a whole. Airline employees still tend to enjoy prestige in their communities because there is a certain romance and excitement about the aviation industry.

THE AIRLINE REVOLUTION

A revolution occurred in the airline industry during the first half of the 1980s. It was triggered by the Airline Deregulation Act of 1978 which gave old and new airlines freedom to fly where they wished and to set fares without government approval. This opened the door to many new low fare carriers such as People Express and spurred widespread fare wars which have put dozens of the newer airlines out of business and threatened the economic health of the older established carriers.

Nevertheless, during the eight years since Congress adopted the deregulation law, the number of scheduled interstate airlines grew from thirty-six to over a hundred. This competition forced the older airlines to reexamine their ways of doing business and led to the following major changes in the industry:

1. Introduction of the two-tier wage which permits an airline to pay new employees less than those who have been working for the company. For example, in one major company an experienced flight attendant earned $31.16 an hour whereas a newly hired employee was paid $21.97.
2. Development of the so-called "hub and spoke routes." This is a new way of scheduling smaller aircraft to cities where there is not enough business to justify using the larger planes. Thus a large plane might fly from Los Angeles to Denver, a hub, where passengers could transfer to one of some four or five connecting flights which will take them (on the spoke routes) to surrounding communities. Wherever this system has been adopted it has opened up new job opportunities in the hub cities, many of which were not previously large employment centers.

3. Growth in the number of mergers between long haul (truck) airlines as well as between long haul and feeder (local service) carriers. Such mergers have reduced the number of companies but usually helped provide better job security for employees of the merging airlines.

The Transportation Research Board, a group of independent experts who advise government agencies, forecast that air travel will grow at the rate of 15 percent annually through the year 2000, with the greatest growth among regional carriers. It is expected that the number of long-haul carriers will decrease to no more than six as airlines merge to become more efficient and offer better service.

This optimistic outlook for a prosperous industry should encourage you to seek your career in this dynamic and growing industry if any aspect of it interests you.

Advertising and public relations personnel develop advertising and promotional materials, including the design, colors, and logos for ticket envelopes, to make their own airline easily distinguishable from others. Photo: Charles Gerity.

CHAPTER 3

MANAGING THE AIRLINE

In the board of directors' room it is exactly ten o'clock and the fifteen men and women take their seats in the office building at the end of the hangar. The walls are paneled in rosewood, concealed lighting gives a soft but adequate amount of light, and a thick carpet creates the sensation of walking on soft moss. The chairperson calls the meeting to order, asks the secretary to give a summary of the minutes of the last meeting and then proceeds to the first item on the agenda. Two hours later the meeting adjourns after the directors have elected a new vice president of sales, approved the purchase of ten Boeing 767 aircraft, ratified a lease with the Port of New York Authority for space in an airport terminal, authorized construction of a new air freight terminal in Houston, and approved a new pension plan for the employees. These men and women who make up the board of directors are the airline's top management. They are elected by the stockholders and without their approval nothing important may be done. Little wonder most of them think that *they are* the airline.

Some six hundred miles west, the three members of a flight crew suddenly become quiet and slightly tense as the aircraft goes into its final descent through stormy clouds. The safe landing depends on how well each does her or his job. These employees are well aware of their importance to the company. Right now *they* are the airline.

Meanwhile, down below and just outside the terminal building the mechanic, hastily summoned to replace a leaking pneumatic tube, expertly fits the new connector in place, only too aware that the flight's on-time departure depends on how quickly he can complete the job. He feels his responsibility and importance at such a time. To him his job—the repair and servicing of an airplane—is the airline.

A reservation clerk downtown is sitting with her headset clamped to her head, her eyes watching the panel in front of her. The instant the red light appears she touches a switch and is connected with a customer who wants to book a seat to Phoenix the next morning. This clerk's working world is the panel with its red light, a copy of the airline schedules, and the small console which looks like a typewriter keyboard and enables her to "talk" with the reservations computer located six hundred miles away. To her these things—the panel, the schedules, and the console—are the airline.

Jeff Rogers, the head porter at Denver, pushes his aluminum luggage carrier into the terminal with two passengers following close behind. He leads them to an empty space at the busy ticket counter where a clerk examines their tickets as Jeff unloads their bags. To Jeff, his luggage rack, the area where cars and taxis stop to discharge the passengers, the traffic of passengers and timing of arrivals and departures, and the lobby of the terminal are the airline.

To the traveling public, on the other hand, the airline is first the reservation clerk who books the flight, then the porter who helps them with luggage, the airport lounge where the tickets are collected, next the cabin of the airplane, and at their destination the baggage pickup room—all of these impressions making up a composite picture of the airline.

When you accept employment and go to work, you too will have a unique conception of what the airline is. Now you will share the thrill of being intimately involved in an exciting business, one of the most dynamic in the country. As you read ahead, imagine yourself working in each of the departments and see which appeals to you—taking into consideration your interests, education, special skills, and goals.

In this chapter we will take a quick walk through the *general office* of an airline. That name is appropriate because the departments which comprise the general office are specialist groups. They serve the entire company rather than carry out a single function. Some general office departments are rather small compared to the finance, sales, operations, flight, and maintenance departments which are directly involved in the day-to-day operation of the company.

In the general office there are fewer job opportunities than elsewhere, and most of them are filled by specialists. Nevertheless there are interesting and well-paid openings for those who have the necessary background and training. There are also positions for clerical personnel including secretaries, stenographers, clerks, and typists.

THE AMERICAN AVIATION DIRECTORY

If you look through the latest issue of the *American Aviation Directory* which lists all the principal officers and departmental directors of every airline, you will discover that no two companies have identical organizations. In one airline the public relations department may report to the president; in another it may be under the vice-president of sales. The flight department in Company A may be one responsibility of the operations vice-president, and in Company B it may have its own vice president. Therefore in this book we shall not follow a single actual airline organization, but we will show how departments are usually organized and where they generally fit into the overall structure of a company. How a particular airline is organized, and just where each department reports, is of little interest until that company is your own company. What is important at this point is to see what each department does and how these activities affect job opportunities. In this chapter a tour of the general office of an airline will suggest the many departmental activities usually found in the headquarters of a major company.

TOP MANAGEMENT

As we get off the elevator on the thirty-second floor of a Chicago office building, the receptionist greets us and announces our arrival to Sheila Barrett, attorney-at-law and Assistant Corporate Secretary, who has been asked to escort us through the four floors of the general offices.

We enter a wide corridor which has five doors on one side and a pair of double doors at the far end. Secretaries are working at desks placed at right angles to the wall beside each of the doors along the hallway. The corridor is quiet, and formally decorated.

"These are the offices of the vice-presidents," Ms. Barrett tells us, "and the last one is the president's office. The other doors at the end of the corridor open into the board of directors' room. I'll admit that these posts are rather distant goals for new employees," our guide observed, "but they are not unattainable. After all, someone has to fill the position of each vice-president and even of the president!"

Her supervising officer, the Vice-President and Corporate Secretary, occupies the office next to the president. The corporate affairs department consists of the Vice-President and Corporate Secretary, Ms. Barrett, and a number of other employees.

CORPORATE AFFAIRS

One of the most important responsibilities of a corporate secretary is attending all meetings of the board of directors and taking the minutes. After each meeting the secretary must write up the minutes and make certain that information about all of the actions approved by the directors is given to the appropriate departments. The purchase of five airplanes, for example, will create a mountain of documents, numerous meetings with representatives of the aircraft manufacturer, and lawyers from both companies. The secretary's office maintains files of all licenses to do business which must be obtained from every state in which the airline operates, as well as all the other certificates and authorizations which are issued by various federal government agencies. Since the minutes of the board of directors contain the authority for everything important which the officers and employees do, the secretary's office is constantly answering questions and being asked to furnish other departments with copies of documents and files.

"So much of a corporate secretary's work is of a legal nature," Ms. Barrett observed, "that it is necessary for the secretary to be a lawyer or for there to be an attorney on the staff." She smiled and added, "There's also another reason and that is to help with the stockholder relations section where there is frequent need for legal advice."

She led us to the floor above, where we stood at one end of a large room watching a dozen employees working with long lists of stockholders' names, examining and filing cards, filling out various forms, and typing letters and lists.

"Many companies employ banks to do this stock transfer work," Ms. Barrett explained, "but we keep our own records here. These men and women handle all the details required to transfer shares of stock when any of our thirty-five thousand stockholders buy or sell the company stock. They also prepare the quarterly dividend checks, make up proxies (voting ballots) for the stockholder meetings, and mail out all of the material which we send to our stockholders from time to time. Actually the company's computer does much of the work for us but all the information has to be prepared and fed into the machine."

She gestured toward the employees who were bent over the desks. "Most of these positions are clerical and call for a knowledge of typing or elementary computer operation. A high school graduate could fill any of these jobs, and after he or she has mastered the work, promotion is possible within the section or to another department. The work is fairly routine but many of our people feel more comfortable in an office where there is no pressure or unexpected crisis. In fact, the tempo of these jobs is like that in the purchasing department which we might visit now since it is just next door."

PURCHASING

"Imagine the variety of items an airline must buy in order to stay in business," the head of the purchasing department said after we had been introduced and sat down in his rather small office. He looked at us and tapped his pencil on his desk as he spoke.

"If you were a purchasing agent here you would have the challenge of spending thousands or perhaps millions of dollars as economically as possible. You and the other buyers would be pricing everything from paper clips, office furniture and calculators to mechanical freight loaders, millions of gallons of kerosene, and multimillion dollar airplanes. The list of items is endless, which is why we have this office as well as branch offices elsewhere in the company."

Each department uses special order forms to requisition the items it needs. Articles such as stationery, cleaning supplies, light bulbs, aircraft tires, and rug runners for use in airplane cabins may be obtained directly from the company warehouses. When some unusual item is needed such as an expensive drawing board, a specially designed ticket counter, or large piece of equipment, the request is sent to the purchasing department and assigned to the purchasing agent who is a specialist in that field.

"Our agents purchase from many sources," the department head continued, "and their responsibility is to find the seller who offers the best value. They may compare listings in catalogs and trade journals before telephoning companies for information. They constantly meet with sales personnel who bring in samples or demonstrate equipment. Usually agents ask two or three suppliers to submit bids on large orders and then award the purchase to the lowest bidder, provided that supplier meets requirements for delivery and quality. In some cases this isn't possible, and an agent must work with one company to obtain some specially designed product. This often calls for technical expertise and is one of the reasons why this work can be so interesting. When planning such a purchase our agent will work with representatives from one or more company departments to make sure that all the necessary specifications are met.

"Once an order is placed, the agent checks frequently to make certain that it will be delivered on time. After the order has been received the agent must see that the equipment, articles, or goods are inspected before payment is authorized.

"A college degree is becoming increasingly important for the employee who hopes to advance to a management position. More and more employers are hiring graduates of associate degree programs in purchasing for beginning jobs," he added, "but regardless of education, an agent must be able to analyze technical data and numbers, and be willing to assume responsibility for spending large sums of money."

A beginning purchasing agent must learn everything possible about the company's business and how the department operates. He or she may be assigned to work with a senior buyer or in the storekeeper's division in order to learn about the inventory system

and storage facilities. After the training period the agent will probably be permitted to purchase catalog or standard items and, as experience is gained, will be given more responsibility and eventually
moved up to a position of assistant purchasing manager in charge of
a group of agents.

Advancement often depends on obtaining additional education.
The designation of Certified Purchasing Manager (CPM) is conferred by the National Association of Purchasing Management, Incorporated, on those who have passed four examinations and met
educational and experience requirements. This CPM indicates that
the individual is experienced and professionally competent, certainly a worthwhile goal for anyone who is interested in making a career
of purchasing.

Mention should also be made of the many openings which exist for
clerical workers in the office and at the storerooms and warehouses.
These employees fill requirements for supplies, keep track of inventory, fill out necessary forms, and reply to correspondence.

THE LIBRARY

Our next stop is a large rectangular room filled with book-
crammed rows of shelves, tables and chairs, and the librarian's desk,
located just inside the door.

"This library serves the entire company," the librarian explained
after we had been introduced. "Our principal function is to provide
information and books on those subjects of the greatest interest to
top management as well as the finance, advertising, public relations,
law, and sales departments. Actually the needs of the maintenance
and operating departments are so specialized—and their offices so
far away—that they have their own files and reference materials.
Many other departments build up their own collections of books and
magazines which relate only to their own activities."

Most airline libraries have no more than one or two librarians and
generally they are graduates of a library science program which calls
for a fifth year of college. Opportunities for librarians are not extensive since there are relatively few aviation libraries and little job

turnover. Don't let this discourage you, however, if you have the training and an airline career interests you. There are openings now and then which occur on a continuing basis.

ADVERTISING

"On the next floor we'll visit the advertising and public relations departments," Ms. Barrett said as she pushed the button for the elevator. A moment later the receptionist on the thirty-fourth floor nodded to us as we passed her desk and then walked down a long narrow corridor to the office of the advertising director. He rose and motioned us to chairs beside his desk.

"Sometimes newspaper advertising seems to be dominated by the airlines," he said, "especially in a large city where several of us compete for business. This makes it difficult for the reader and would-be traveler to distinguish between companies. You've probably noticed that most airlines depart at 'convenient hours,' most boast of 'on-time arrivals,' most serve steak or lobster, show movies, and fly the same type of equipment. The questions are: how do they differ, which is best, and how do we tell the public in such a way that it remembers our airline?"

Not waiting for us to attempt to answer his questions, he continued: "How does an advertising director make certain his advertising is winning riders to his airline?" He then told us a story about Bert Lynn, director of advertising for Western Air Lines who faced this problem.

One evening Lynn was watching an animated cartoon on television which advertised the Bank of America. He had an idea. The next morning he asked Western's advertising agency to find out who produced the cartoon. Shortly thereafter he called Storybook, Incorporated, and talked with the producer about his inspiration.

A month later he had a call from Storybook. "We've got something to show you now, Mr. Lynn. Can you come over?"

An hour later Lynn and Art Kelly, Vice-President-Sales, were watching a bird which resembled a parrot sitting on top of an airplane in front of the tail. A voice on the sound track announced in a deep tone: "Western—the only way to fly."

The idea was certainly different the two men agreed, but was it too cute, too ridiculous, too different? More important, would it persuade people to fly Western?

The VIB—"Very Important Bird"—which Lynn and Kelly saw that morning worked for Western for thirteen years before it was retired: a retirement that proved premature. Fan mail continued to pour in and the little bird returned to the screen while its slogan: "The only way to fly" was mentioned by many movie stars and others in the entertainment world. Astronaut James Lovell, while he was sitting in his space capsule orbiting the earth, quoted the bird and told millions watching him, "It's the only way to fly!"

"Now, we must admit that few advertising campaigns achieve such success," the director continued, "but everyone in an airline advertising department hopes to come up with just the right slogan or gimmick which will focus attention on the company. That's the challenge—that's the fun of it all—and once in a while a great idea is the icing on the cake." He leaned forward and looked at us intently as he said: "Actually, though, most airlines rely on one of the more prominent advertising agencies to handle their programs and dream up unusual ad ideas."

He then explained that an airline's advertising department is usually responsible for supervising what the advertising agency does, planning advertising campaigns, deciding where the ads will be placed, and coordinating the advertising programs with the sales department which has the greatest interest in how the company advertises. Therefore this may not be a very large department, especially if the advertising agency prepares the ads and sends them out to the newspapers, magazines, radio, and television stations.

If advertising excites you and you want to work in the airline field, your best move would be to obtain a job in an advertising agency which has an aviation account and do everything possible to get yourself assigned to that airline. Some employers seek college graduates with degrees in business with an emphasis on advertising or marketing. Others prefer a liberal arts background with social science, literature, art, and other disciplines in your record. Still others place little or no emphasis on the type of degree. In some firms you start as a specialist and do not gain all-around experience, in others you may begin as a research or production assistant, a space or time buyer, or even a junior copywriter.

If you are creative, talented, and work hard, this could be a satisfying career for you. As a copywriter or account executive you might advance to better positions, become a partner in the agency, or perhaps be asked by a client to head its advertising department. For many people the satisfaction comes from having their work appear on television, radio, or in print even though their names are never associated with the advertising and remain unknown to the public.

PUBLIC RELATIONS

The rest of the thirty-fourth floor is occupied by the headquarters office of the public relations department. Public relations in its very broadest sense is dealing successfully with people, but this definition is not quite complete because it might imply a selfish motive designed to bring unconscionable gain. If, on the other hand, we say that public relations is dealing successfully with people with the emphasis on an activity that is beneficial to the public or that endeavors to gain the good will and understanding of the public, it has a real purpose and objective.

Most airlines have strong public relations departments because it is important that they project the best possible public image. Public relations is more than telling the boss's story, however. An important part of the job is understanding the concerns and attitudes of customers, company employees, politicians, and other "publics" and conveying this information effectively to the management.

Ms. Barrett introduced us to Tony Romano, Director of Public Relations, who is responsible for coordinating all of the departmental activities and acting as a go-between, or liaison, between the department and other groups in the company.

"Let me take you around the office," he said, "and quickly point out the various functions and responsibilities. Bear in mind, though," he warned us, "no two airlines organize their public relations departments alike although we all do pretty much the same things."

We stopped at the door to an office on which there was the title: "Manager of Press Relations." The office was dark, indicating that the manager was away.

"This person is responsible for maintaining the best possible relations with the press which entails cultivating a friendship with the aviation editors of leading newspapers and magazines because when the top management wants to get a message to the public, we must rely on these editors to accept the story and print it. Furthermore, when bad news gets into the newspapers—an accident, an unfavorable government report, a lawsuit—it is helpful to have editors who will report the event truthfully and perhaps come to us for additional facts or an explanation, rather than slant the story against us."

We moved on to the next office in which a woman was busy at her typewriter. After a brief introduction Mr. Romano explained that the duties of this special features editor were to prepare originaï news stories about women flight attendants, women reservations agents, and other female employees. "What she writes will be of interest to editors of women's pages in newspapers and magazines," he said. "She is also available for consultation when a writer needs information for an article or book about airlines or airline personnel."

After chatting with this editor we continued our tour, talking briefly with a research worker who prepares material for outsiders or employees who need special information, another woman who handles all the contacts with employee organizations, a man who edits a weekly newsletter for employees, a speechwriter who does nothing but write speeches for members of the management, a woman who spends all her time arranging for publicity tie-ins (such as having a picture of the company's planes displayed on a box of cereal), an office manager who somehow keeps the busy office functioning, and several stenographers and secretaries who work for the various members of the department.

"Everyone here is busy telling others about our airline," Mr. Romano observed, "but when there is an accident, our public relations machinery goes quickly into reverse. Then, instead of trying to obtain attention, we do all we can to tone down newspaper, radio, and television coverage of the disaster. Accidents are front page news; we can't keep the stories out of the newspapers but we work with the press to do everything possible to see that the stories are accurate and free from rumors or sensationalism."

At such times all members of the department may work steadily for a week or longer with little sleep as they answer questions, assist families of the injured or deceased, obtain obituaries of the dead, and handle a thousand unexpected problems which invariably turn up.

In some companies one or two employees may comprise the entire public relations staff while in others there may be a dozen or more employees. There is wide variation in the ways that companies handle their public relations. Most of them try to cooperate with the public and the press to the best of their ability. However, there have been and still are some company executives who will reply: "No comment," when asked a question about a sensitive matter.

A recent survey revealed that "probably two-thirds of the public relations employees had no course work in the field." Nevertheless many men and women enter the public relations practice directly from college and a college education is considered necessary to succeed in this field. Good training for one interested in making this a career may be obtained at a school of journalism or public relations. According to a guide issued by the Public Relations Society of America, the person interested in entering public relations should focus on liberal arts and humanities with some courses on public relations and communications. It is also still possible to obtain some newspaper background after graduation and then switch to public relations.

Prospects for a successful career in public relations are greatest for those who have prepared themselves adequately in college.

SECURITY

The door to the security department was locked; investigators were out in the field and the department head was elsewhere in the building.

"Airlines have security problems the same as other companies," Ms. Barrett told us. "We employ guards at airports, hangars, offices, in fact wherever there is need to protect people, equipment, or property from criminal activity. Warehouses and loading dock areas where air freight and mail are stored and transferred to and from trucks also need protection."

She then explained that some companies contract with agencies like Pinkerton or Holmes for their guards while others hire their own. Retired policemen and military personnel are often sought but it is not unusual for young men and women without prior experience to be hired and trained for security positions.

In many companies the term *security* includes another, but different function: auditing all the company accounts. This involves examining all records pertaining to ticket sales, cash accounts, and other corporate financial records to make certain that the accounts are accurate and that money has not been embezzled by dishonest employees or outsiders. Expert accountants are hired for this job, men and women who have majored in accounting at college and have had prior financial experience. Sometimes former FBI agents are also employed.

MAIL SERVICE

Behind the door marked "Mail Services" was a large room with letterboxes, as in a post office, across one wall. Along the other three walls were counters where mail was being sorted into piles or put into large canvas bags. Ms. Jackson, the department head, greeted us and began to tell us about her department.

"Since every office in this company receives and sends mail, we need a lot of people to pick up outgoing mail from each office location, as well as to deliver incoming letters." She glanced about the room and pointed to some young men who were sorting envelopes into the mailboxes. "This is like a miniature post office, but there is a difference. In addition to regular mail, we have our own internal office mail which must be delivered quickly between every company office in the country." Pointing to a map of the airline system which hung on the wall above the postage meter machine, she added: "You can appreciate what a job this is since we have so many ticket offices, reservations offices, airports, maintenance bases, and other installations. And," she added, "everybody expects overnight delivery!"

Most of the mail which is sent between offices is carried on company planes as "company mail" and this means that mailbags must be dispatched between every office, creating an intricate network of intracompany mail deliveries.

All of this activity calls for mail supervisors at various offices as well as numerous clerks to handle the large volume of mail. Most of these employees are young men and women who have recently graduated from high school. The mail department of any airline is a good place to start an airline career if an individual does not have any special skill. It is possible to earn promotion to supervisory or a specialist position or transfer to other departments. Many members of management are proud to admit that they started their careers in the mail room.

PUBLICATIONS

Next, Ms. Barrett led us into a noisy area which looked like a printing plant. A number of different machines were spewing out bulletins, memoranda, newsletters—all kinds of printed material. At one side of the room a half-dozen women and men were typing on stencils and duplicating masters while others were operating mimeograph, multigraph, and offset machines. Six employees stood at a long table collating stacks of paper into piles which were inserted in loose-leaf binders.

"We use a lot of typists here," the manager told us as he wiped his hands on his apron. It was difficult to hear him above the din of the typewriters and other machines. "Our people are so good that other departments often ask for them when they have vacancies and we're always glad to see them promoted, but of course it means hiring others to replace them."

"Is this also true for the other employees?" we asked.

"Not much, I'm sorry to say, because there aren't other jobs which can use these same skills. A good machine operator here might apply for a mechanic's job and receive favorable consideration, but the collators and others would probably have to start elsewhere in beginning clerical positions. Word processor operators are in demand."

"What experience do your machine operators need?"

"Many of them have had office training in high school or in a business school," he replied. "Some transfer from mail services and we train them. There is no special training or experience required if a person is interested in learning the job. We can train the person to operate what is really a fairly simple machine." He smiled as he shoved his hands into his apron pockets. "You can understand why we have a higher turnover than most departments—but then, that spells opportunity for those who work here, although it means extra problems for me."

As we returned to the mail room it was suddenly obvious why the publications department was located next door. Since all the printed materials had to be sent somewhere in the company, it was very convenient to be adjacent to the mail department.

COMMUNITY RELATIONS

In some companies community relations is part of public relations; in others it is a separate department. In either case community relations is a special kind of public relations which usually concentrates on working with the civic and political leaders in the communities served by the airline.

One of the responsibilities of department members is to be available to state legislators as well as members of Congress to explain the airline's position on proposed legislation which might affect the company in one way or another. They may actually engage in lobbying; that is, attempting to secure passage or rejection of legislation by influencing legislators or public officials. At the same time members of the community relations department emphasize to these political leaders that they will help them or their staffs in every possible way should they need certain information. Another duty of the departmental members is to participate in various community activities such as helping to organize community programs, work on charitable drives, direct special civic projects, or recruit company employees to help with community projects. The department also gives the airline's city managers advice and help in solving those local problems which involve civic or political matters.

This work is interesting, demanding, and calls for individuals who know how to work with people and who understand politics. They must be willing to remain in the background, content to let others take credit for whatever they may accomplish. A college education and several years experience in the industry are usually required for one of these positions. Thus it is a job to work toward rather than seek as a newcomer.

LEGAL SERVICES

With Ms. Barrett we entered the law library, a room lined with well-filled bookcases. Two large tables and several comfortable chairs completed the furnishings. Doors opened from the law library to the offices of each attorney.

Ms. Barrett motioned us to the nearby chairs, and said, "I'll take a few minutes to tell you about the department. Most airlines require extensive legal services and many have law departments like ours in addition to using the services of outside law firms. Our lawyers are kept busy interpreting government laws and regulations, representing the company in law suits, considering the legality of proposed financial arrangements, drafting contracts for leasing or buying aircraft, deciding on the legality of new fares, filing applications for permits of various kinds, as well as counseling top management on legal matters. Sounds impressive, doesn't it?" She smiled, and we nodded in agreement.

She then pointed out that the lawyers are expected to know everything about an airline. At one time it even seemed one had to be a lawyer in order to become an executive—so important was a legal training considered. That is no longer the case although it is a great advantage to have a law degree. Lawyers are valuable to a company because they have had special training which prepares them to solve problems cautiously and logically. Lawyers are not necessarily prepared to think up clever sales promotion programs or decide on how best to ticket a passenger, but they can determine whether or not what is planned is legal and whether it will fit into the company's overall policy. Good lawyers should achieve success in an airline even though their eventual position may involve much more than working on legal problems.

Aviation law is a specialized field. Although the job market for lawyers expands and contracts, there are often openings for promising lawyers, especially if they come from one of the more prestigious law schools.

"A young person should not despair if he or she did not attend one of the top law schools," Ms. Barrett said. "It is still possible to find a job, but it may not be easy. I think the best entrée into aviation is to clerk in a law firm whose clients include a number of large or medium-size corporations including an airline. A law school graduate should apply for a job as a law clerk or research assistant. Later it may be possible to be assigned to work in the law firm's office at the airline or to try for a position in the airline's legal department."

She rose from her chair, and as she walked toward the door, turned and added: "Lawyers are as necessary to an airline as pilots—and they can make almost as much money!"

CORPORATE COMMUNICATIONS

"Meet Maria Perez, our chief operator," Ms. Barrett said as we stood by the long switchboard and watched the three operators expertly answer a constant stream of incoming telephone calls. It was fascinating to see the lights blink on and off as the operators handled each call seemingly with no effort.

Ms. Perez explained: "There are four of us and we rotate so that one of us can be on a break. This work is very tiring when the board is busy and you need a rest now and then. If the board gets terribly busy—after a strike, an accident, or something unusual—then you'll find the four of us here most of the time."

The work of a switchboard operator was much heavier before the advent of direct dialing. This enables anyone to call an extension in the company without going through the switchboard operators.

Employees may also dial calls to telephones outside the company without an operator's assistance.

"All these calls you see are from people who don't know which extension to dial," Ms. Perez said, as she pointed to the switchboard. "Most of them need our help in deciding who in the company can help them."

Ms. Perez then observed that it calls for a thorough knowledge of the company and the various departments to operate a large company switchboard. The operators must know where they can reach every employee as well as who does what, so they can refer calls quickly and accurately. There are switchboards all over the company wherever there are large numbers of telephones and incoming calls from the public.

Operating a switchboard requires patience, quick thinking, a good memory, a clear voice and pleasing manner, and as Ms. Perez said, a knowledge of the company. Business courses in high school and some other schools often include instruction for those who want to become operators and many companies give on-the-job training.

In most airlines telephone operations come under the coordination of the communications department. A telecommunications company usually installs and maintains the telephone system but it is necessary for the airline to plan telephone needs in advance and work with the phone company representatives. This planning may call for engineers capable of making forecasts of future communications traffic loads, analyzing them, and deciding what and how much equipment will be required to meet the demands. This is especially true in the reservations department where increasing passenger loads (usually caused by lower fares or national prosperity) can create heavy demands for additional reservations clerks—and that means more telephones and related equipment.

In addition there are other intracompany communications systems, notably teletype and radio contact between flight crews and ground dispatchers and others who keep in touch with the planes. This calls for the services of radio technicians and communications specialists who have been trained in college, vocational or technical schools, or who may have received their training and experience with one of the telephone companies before coming to work for an airline.

The communications field changes rapidly with technological innovations; therefore, if this area interests you, you should contact the personnel offices of two or three airlines and find out about their needs and the experience and education they are seeking for their positions. This is not likely to be a large department but none is more vital—for without the ability to communicate quickly and reliably—an airline cannot operate.

DATA PROCESSING

We might say this is the heart of the company, the place where valuable information is stored and is available when needed," said Ms. Barrett. "It was only 1951 when the first computer was installed for commercial use and our ways of doing business since then have been revolutionized. Today we use computers to keep stockholder records and print dividend checks, prepare the company payroll, keep personnel records, do accounting work, prepare purchasing information and keep inventories of hundreds of items, to say nothing of processing flight records. Besides this computer, there is another which keeps the reservation records and prepares all the information needed about the number of seats sold on every flight."

She held the door open for us and continued:

"I have had to learn a lot about computers since all our stockholder records are processed here. In fact, I would advise young people who plan a business career to learn everything they can about computers and how they work. After all, most businesses are becoming more and more dependent on them."

A recent survey of airlines reveals the extensive use now made of computers.

Reservations Department: ticket and travel agents (worldwide) have instant access to the central computer of many airlines to obtain information about schedules, reservations, interline connections, check-ins, rates, flights, hotel and rental car information, and baggage tracing. The computer can also print tickets instantly.

Operations Department: the computer is used to do the necessary calculations for crew management, flight planning, fuel consumption, and weight balance for each flight.

Maintenance Department: the computer keeps inventory records, schedules when each airplane must go for a certain type of maintenance, and keeps the maintenance records of each plane.

Miscellaneous: the computer performs tasks such as compiling and analyzing financial and sales records, preparing payroll records and paychecks, handling cargo and stock control, preparing government reports and keeping stockholder and personnel records, as well as many other types of information needed by management.

Now back to our tour. We were in an office where a number of data typists were seated in front of small screens with typewriter keys below them. As they typed each letter or numeral, it appeared on the screen while electrical impulses fed the data directly into the computer or stored it on a tape or disc.

She pointed to a woman working next to several metal cabinets which had numerous discs stored in them. "She is the tape librarian," Ms. Barrett observed. "She classifies and catalogs all information which has been put on tapes or discs and is important enough to be kept for future use or reference. Thanks to her cataloging, the material is easy to find when you need it."

It would appear that the data typists might be bored inasmuch as they do nothing but type at their machines all day, and Ms. Barrett admitted that this work was repetitious and appealed only to certain people. Promotion is limited, although advancement to a supervisory position is possible after a number of years and some employees who obtain additional training may gain jobs as programmers or console operators.

Our guide motioned us to where we could look through a large picture window into another room filled with green metal cabinets, in some of which we could see discs revolving.

"That's the computer room," she said. "The console operators usually are the only employees permitted in there. Console operators need several months of training for this job. They study the instructions for processing whatever data is to go into the computer (which is called input), load the discs or magnetic tapes into the computer, and start the machine. Operators must be alert while the console is running to see that nothing goes wrong. Error lights will signal a malfunction and the operators must know how to locate and repair the trouble. Good console operators can trace the causes of failures but this knowledge is not gained quickly. With experience, operators can move up eventually to supervisory posts or to related jobs as programmers.

"What do the programmers do?" we asked, this being an entirely new area.

"Programmers are important to the successful operation of a computer because they feed it the necessary step-by-step instructions to be followed. The machine has no brain so it must be given detailed directions which are called programs. The programmers list the steps the machine must take to solve problems or produce the desired information."

A programmer writes in a special language which has been developed especially for computers and each program is different. The instructions required to tell the computer how to process a complicated payroll will be entirely different from those telling the machine how to bill customers, calculate finance charges, add charges, deduct payments, and prepare monthly statements.

"Most programmers are college graduates and those who make the programs for engineering or scientific applications usually need graduate degrees in computer science, engineering, mathematics, or in the physical sciences," the lawyer said. "For airlines I would say that college courses in data processing, accounting and business administration would be desirable background. Programming is taught in all types of schools from high school to colleges and universities. Ingenuity, imagination, logic, patience, persistence, and accuracy are the principal qualifications required for the work."

The next position above that of computer programmer is systems analyst—a man or woman who discusses a data processing problem with a departmental manager or specialist. After the analyst learns the exact nature of the problem it must be decided how to use the computer to solve it. Prior work experience is necessary, and therefore this is a good job for young people to work toward after they have mastered other positions in the computer field.

Computerized data processing facilitates all areas of airline operations, including managing passenger reservations, accounting, and flight information. Photo: American Airlines.

When we left the department and walked toward the elevators, Ms. Barrett added: "Computers are here to stay, so it is a good end of the business for a young person to learn—in fact it is as exciting and promising in its way as aviation!"

As we returned to the room where the receptionist sat, Ms. Barrett realized that she had not mentioned this position. The company employs receptionists in many offices and while no specific qualifications are required for the job, a knowledge of typing is useful and may help a young person gain employment. Some receptionists also operate a small switchboard, type, file, and perform other assignments. Because the receptionist is often the first person in a company whom the public meets, careful grooming and pleasantness of manner are extremely important. Although there is normally little opportunity for advancement, a receptionist who has typing, shorthand, or bookkeeping skills can usually transfer to other positions as they become available.

We thanked our guide, said goodbye, then sped down to the ground floor and walked out on the busy street. In thinking back over the tour we realized that the general offices of an airline offer as wide a variety of job opportunities as can be found in the offices of most large companies. We had by no means exhausted the possibilities for employment: there were still all those jobs in sales, reservations, maintenance, flight, and other departments which will be covered in the following chapters.

Passenger ticket sales represent a substantial portion of airline finances; therefore, careful handling of each ticket sale and courtesy to each passenger is essential. Photo: American Airlines.

CHAPTER 4

THE FINANCE DEPARTMENT

When Colonial Airlines started operating between New Jersey and Boston in 1926, the treasurer had an easy job. Cash came from three sources: the two airport ticket offices at either end of the route and the Post Office Department which paid the company monthly for each pound of mail it carried. Expenses consisted of salaries for the few airport employees and crew members, rental of space at the two airports, gasoline and oil, aircraft spare parts, and office supplies.

Today a large airline may take in over two million dollars a day and spend most of it. In fact so much money flows into the many company bank accounts that it is not unusual for an officer to be responsible only for transferring the extra cash daily from one bank to another to earn as much interest as possible. An airline may maintain one or more bank accounts in every city it serves. Few people are aware of what the finance department does although it is one of the most important and complex divisions of any airline.

Not everyone is attracted to a career in finance and this may be a department you have not considered. You may not like the idea of working with figures all your life, and may have little aptitude for them. If this is your honest and accurate opinion, by all means consider other types of work. However, may we suggest that you at least keep an open mind and read this chapter, if for no other reason than to have an idea of what an airline finance department does. The world of finance—be it with a bank, the government, a corporation, a college, or any other large organization—can be quite fascinating and rewarding.

Although the functions of the various sections of an airline finance department vary greatly and bear little resemblance to each other, the entry jobs and many of the skills required at all levels for each section are similar.

Accountants, accounting clerks, bookkeepers, filing clerks, lawyers, managers, secretaries, and typists are the principal job titles you will find in a finance department. The challenge and interest come from the fact that regardless of your starting position, as you earn promotion your work will probably become more and more specialized. Thus you might start as an accountant, a bookkeeper, or a clerk doing routine work, and end up as a specialist in budgets, the tax department, a pension consultant, or a supervisor in any one of the other sections.

As you will see, the work of a finance department is not necessarily just statistical reports, balance sheets, or profit and loss statements. In some companies the finance division may also be concerned with insurance, tax administration, and budgets if these functions do not fit into other areas of the organization.

Rather than repeat the job duties in each of the various sections we will give a quick overview of what the people in this department do. This will enable you to see the breadth of opportunity which exists here, and if a career in finance interests you, permit you to visualize where you might fit in this part of the airline business.

REVENUE ACCOUNTING AND DISBURSEMENTS

Perhaps the two most important sections of a finance department are those which receive and spend the money: revenue accounting and disbursements. To give you an idea of where the money comes from and what the revenue accounting section does, here are the principal sources from which the large amounts of cash come, seven days a week, fifty-two weeks a year:

- more than a hundred and fifty ticket offices, and as many airport freight depots and ticket offices.
- thousands of travel agents.

- every other airline in the United States and throughout the world.
- freight forwarders who pick up and ship freight.
- finance companies which issue credit cards used to purchase airline tickets.
- the United States Post Office and other carriers which contract with airlines to fly much of the mail, and other packages.

An endless stream of money pours into the company daily from each of these sources and every dollar must be accounted for, just as the records of printed tickets and waybills must be audited constantly lest any fall into the hands of unauthorized people. The actual organization of the revenue accounting section may vary from company to company but the nature of the work performed is the same: the accuracy of all records covering the sale of tickets and deposits of cash must be verified, and daily reports of all income received must be compiled. Needless to say, auditing the tickets, waybills, and other documents which are prepared by ticket offices, freight offices, travel agents, and others can be a complicated job.

A passenger may buy a ticket on Airline A for a flight from New York to Chicago but for some reason decide to fly on Airline B which honors the ticket. This means that although Airline A received the money for the ticket, once Airline B has flown the passenger it must collect the fare from Airline A. This calls for a special procedure which is routine between airlines but nevertheless must be checked and accounted for by revenue accounting.

It is also common for an airline to book a passenger for a trip which will involve passage over its own routes as well as routes of one or more other airlines. The airline which prepares the ticket collects all the money from the passenger and then must arrange to pay the other airlines for their portions of the trip. Every day millions of dollars are exchanged between airlines because many tickets are sold in this manner. To make the task easier the airlines operate a clearing-house which transfers the money and notifies the airlines of the amounts due them from each such transaction.

There is no such clearing-house to help the disbursements section which is responsible for paying all the bills which have been authorized by numerous employees as well as the purchasing department.

Hundreds of checks may be prepared each day as a huge amount of paperwork is processed. Thus some employees are busy just receiving the payment requests (also called vouchers) and putting them in order to give to other employees. These people will make sure that each request has the proper approvals and does not exceed the dollar amount allowed for its category. (Company regulations usually show the maximum amount each level of management may approve for spending.) Another group of clerks checks the discounts* and does the necessary statistical work to determine the final amount to be paid, whereupon the checks must go through a check-writing machine which imprints the amount on each. Finally each of the vouchers containing a carbon copy of the check and other papers must be stapled together and filed. At the same time a list of payments must be prepared and coded so that the general accounting office will know where to charge each check drawn.

GENERAL ACCOUNTING

Someone has to put together the records of all money received and spent and keep track of cash on hand. The general accounting section does this. The comprehensive records which these accountants maintain are the basis for the profit and loss statement, all types of expense reports, departmental budgets, income tax returns, and other reports which must be filed with various government agencies by this section.

PAYROLL

The payroll section issues all payroll checks—a big order, especially if there are many thousands of employees. Dates when employees are paid must be staggered so that the work is spread out over the month. Although most checks are prepared by computer, again it is the human being who must instruct the computer regarding the indi-

---

*Some companies offer a 1 or 2 percent discount if the bill is paid within ten days.

vidual amounts, after figuring the various deductions for each employee. As if this were not enough work, there are always those employees who lose their checks and need duplicates, those going on vacation who request salary advances, those who are dismissed suddenly and must be given the money due them, and any temporary workers who may be on the payroll for only short periods of time.

The work of the four sections described above is essentially of a routine accounting nature which can have a real fascination for those with statistical or accounting interests. The responsibilities of the sections covered below are quite specialized and not strictly of an accounting nature (although bookkeeping and accounting are essential in each), and could prove extremely rewarding if you were to make one of them your career.

INSURANCE

The insurance section is responsible for placing all company insurance, paying premiums, filing claims, and keeping all necessary records. The largest insurance policies are those which cover the aircraft, coverage which can amount to hundreds of millions of dollars. More importantly insurance is purchased to take care of any passenger injuries or fatalities. Today a serious accident may involve hundreds of people, including passengers and crew members and perhaps other persons on the ground; and although it can create a nightmare for everyone involved, the company as a whole usually does not suffer extreme financial catastrophe if the insurance section has done its job properly.

In addition, all types of insurance policies must be written to provide protection for company property against fire and theft, for employees against injuries incurred while on duty, and for the public against any accidents they might experience while they are on company property.

Generally a broker places the insurance with various underwriters, but someone in the airline must direct the broker and be responsible for seeing that adequate insurance of all kinds is in force. The insurance section must also investigate all claims and keep detailed records relating to accidents or other problems which may involve a potential settlement by an insurance company. This calls for specialists who either learn on the job over the years and gradually grow into more responsible positions, or men and women who have had special training in all phases of insurance at college.

TAX ADMINISTRATION

Corporation tax laws change frequently and are so complicated that only a person who has specialized in tax matters can interpret tax legislation and decide efficiently how the company can best plan its financial affairs and operating policies in order to minimize its taxes and take advantage of all the special exemptions provided by law. Companies pay millions of dollars in taxes and therefore it is important that the tax section be staffed with the best experts available.

An airline which operates in several states may be liable for taxes to each of the states as well as to some of the cities which it serves. Because of this, the tax section must know about every possible tax which has been levied against the company in every locality it serves. For example, the tax section may decide that it would be advantageous from a tax point of view to buy all airplane fuel only in certain states. Although this would save money it would require rescheduling aircraft so that they would no longer fuel in the states which charge higher fuel taxes. In some places city and state sales taxes may make it necessary to avoid buying expensive equipment. When selling airplanes it may be necessary to fly them several thousand miles to a remote airport in a state where there are no taxes imposed on such a sale.

Essentially the tax experts are responsible for keeping up-to-date on all tax laws—federal, state, county, and municipal —to make certain that everything is done to keep the airline's tax bill as low as possible. These men and women can save the company millions of dollars and earn their salaries many times over. You can see why the tax section is so important in today's economy.

If this work sounds interesting you should consider going to graduate business school or at least taking as many courses in business, finance, and taxes as you can in college. Ideally the best-prepared tax experts are those who have a Master of Business Administration as well as a law degree. This is more education than many young men and women can afford but it is possible to obtain your legal education at night school, an achievement which, though it can require six or seven years, is one way of preparing thoroughly for the job. Competent tax experts will always be in demand, hence it will be a very worthwhile educational investment.

BUDGET

If you budget your personal income and expenses you know what a tremendous help it is in planning for your financial future. Budgeting is just as important to any business because if it is to be successful there must be a plan or statement of its financial position for a definite period of time based on estimates of its income and expenditures. A good budget shows how much money is expected to be available for certain listed expenses and where that money will come from. In an airline a budget section may report directly to the president or be part of the finance department on which it must rely for much of its financial information.

An annual airline budget is prepared by estimating what the income will be for the coming year from passenger, freight, and mail revenues. These estimates are prepared by economists who study business trends, economic indicators, and other data to come up with the best possible forecast of how much business the airline will do.

To determine what future expenses an airline company will have, every department is required to submit a detailed budget for the coming year which shows salaries and every other kind of expense, as well as how much any expense has increased over the past year and why. The budget section then matches the estimated income with the total projected departmental expenses and the difference tells the expected profit or loss. If it is a loss each department may be

Accounting procedures for an airline are basically the same as for any other kind of business. Photo: Illinois CPA Society.

instructed to cut its expenses by a certain percentage so that the red ink can be turned into black. The budget section watches all expenditures during the next year and prepares monthly reports for each department to show how well it adhered to its budget. Most departments have their own budget supervisor who prepares and administers the departmental budget.

The work of this section is critical. The financial health of the airline may depend on how well these specialists do their jobs estimating income and monitoring the expenses as the year progresses. Thus the section is busy keeping statistics on all departments, revising income estimates, watching expenditures, and reporting when expenses get out of line.

The responsibility for projecting income and expenses is certainly the most challenging part of this work and one which calls for the skills of competent economists. A broad knowledge of economics as well as an understanding of the airline business in general is vital. Economists with a Master of Business Administration degree are ideal candidates for working in this department. As with the tax experts, economists who chalk up good records are always able to find employment.

It is impossible to describe here the many clerical and bookkeeping positions which may be found in the finance department. Accounting clerks, sometimes called bookkeeping clerks, perform a variety of routine duties which may include recording details of business transactions; filing; typing vouchers, invoices, and other financial documents; posting accounts; computing data; checking the work of others for accuracy; and compiling reports. Some of these positions require typewriting ability, others call for legible handwriting. As computers are more widely used there is less need to post records by hand in accounting departments.

The work in many clerical and accounting positions is repetitive and may not be especially stimulating. This need not discourage you if you are looking forward to a long career. Once you have demonstrated ability and have worked on the same job for a reasonable time, you can request a transfer if you feel you are in a dead-end job.

The sales department has overall responsibility for courteous service to customers, not only by phone but also in person at the terminal. Photo: United Airlines.

CHAPTER 5

THE SALES DEPARTMENT

Henry Van Orsdale arrived just before the regular Monday morning sales meeting adjourned.

"Sorry to be so late, Dick," he told Richard Stein, the District Sales Manager, as he sat down. "Stanley Hollingsworth and his staff left on Flight 62 for Phoenix and I couldn't get away any sooner." The sales manager nodded and smiled, knowing that when Stanley Hollingsworth took a dozen top staff members anywhere for a meeting, he expected red carpet treatment and that Henry would be on hand to see that their reservations were in order.

"That's our most important Boston account," Stein said. "I guess you've been servicing them for over twenty-five years. Keep up the good work, we can't afford to lose their business to anyone else!"

SALES REPRESENTATIVES

Several men and women were meeting in the airline's offices on Boston's State Street. In addition to the manager there were Mary Minton, Sally Ramirez, and Henry Van Orsdale, the passenger sales representatives, Tom Poulos, the freight sales representative, and Eugene Logan, the agency representative. This particular office is responsible for sales in the Boston area as well as all of Massachusetts, Vermont, New Hampshire, and Maine, a territory Logan covered. On the road five days a week, he calls at every travel agency in the four states, except Boston, making the rounds about three times a year. He is the company representative the head of a travel agency would contact if there were problems; he is the one who urges agencies to book their business on his airline rather than with competitors; and he is the one who sees to it that the important agencies which give him the most business have access to special reservations people who handle their requests. He enjoys his job because he is his own boss and not tied down to an office.

Each of the three passenger representatives is assigned a number of large companies or organizations—known as "accounts"—to be called on regularly. In some companies a transportation or traffic manager handles all requests for air reservations. In these cases the airline sales representative needs to contact only one person, but in those firms which have no traffic manager, it may be necessary to keep in touch with the executives' secretaries as well as some management personnel in order to make certain of keeping in contact and keeping their patronage.

Tom Poulos' task is a bit more difficult because he is the only air freight salesman in the region and there is a lot to do. He calls regularly on the major shippers in the Boston area, visits new companies which might use the airline's air freight service, and is available to help expedite an emergency shipment, trace a lost shipment, or soothe an irate customer if an airplane is delayed for some reason. He likes his job because he enjoys working with people, and finds it challenging to try and discover ways that air freight can be used to save a company money.

Mary Minton started her career after college as a reservations agent. She then won promotion to the ticket counter and eventually became a passenger service representative. Mr. Stein had noticed how professionally this efficient woman handled difficult situations, and when there was an opening on the sales staff he offered her the job. Customers discovered that she was knowledgeable and helpful and soon welcomed her visits.

As a sales representative it is her responsibility to call on prospective customers (mostly large companies) to stimulate business and vacation travel, to explain the advantages of her airline's service for travel and shipping freight, to tell about new promotional fares and services, and to offer her assistance in handling difficult reservations or even making occasional hotel reservations. She also keeps in touch with certain travel agencies in Boston as well as larger charitable and educational institutions which use the airline's service. She and the other two sales representatives share responsibility for making frequent visits at the offices of other airlines in order to remind them that each should sell the other's service whenever possible. This can be done whenever a passenger wants to take a trip which involves travel over several airlines.

At one time experience working in reservations or ticket offices was necessary to qualify for the job of sales representative. While reservations or ticket agents occasionally still win promotion to the sales force, many airlines are now looking for men and women who have college degrees with courses in air transportation management. It is also helpful to have studied psychology, public speaking, and sales techniques. On-the-job training may be given and some airlines hire college students during summer vacation periods for training, then appoint them as "campus representatives" on their return to college. In this post they contact faculty members and students to tell them about the airline's services and special holiday trip offers. These part-time jobs sometimes lead to full-time positions after graduation from college.

The sales department of an airline is unlike that of most companies. Many salespeople for manufacturers, for example, are paid commissions on what they sell or they may receive a salary plus commissions. Airline sales representatives have a different situation, however. They do not sell tickets and they rarely handle reservations themselves but instead concentrate their efforts on influencing customers to patronize their airline. It would be impossible to trace actual sales to their efforts since most airline seats are sold over the telephone, at ticket offices, or through travel agents. For this reason airline sales representatives receive a straight salary.

It is the responsibility of the sales department to see that the company's airplane seats and cargo space on every flight are filled with bodies and freight. Space, be it an airplane seat or the cargo hold in the lower part of the fuselage, is a "perishable" commodity. A company which makes toothbrushes can keep the brushes in its warehouse until its sales personnel write orders for them. In the airline business, though, once a plane leaves the terminal, every unoccupied seat is empty space which must be carried to the next stop. On a transcontinental flight where the fare is $250, for example, twenty empty seats represent a loss of $5,000 worth of potential revenue, $5,000 which will not be recovered because that flight can never be flown again.

SALES ADMINISTRATION

The administrative office of the sales department directs the overall operation of the department, plans the sales programs, and makes certain they are followed by all sales offices. There may be several directors of sales divisions who work under the vice president of sales. Each director probably has a small staff of assistants and specialists.

One of the most important events in a sales department is the annual sales meeting when all of the division directors present their programs for the coming year together with the sales' goals and expected sales increases. Sometimes a company-wide sales meeting is held in a resort where all the city, district, and regional sales managers gather for a two or three day meeting which is a combination pep, planning, and socializing session. Some companies shun holding a large meeting and have "road companies" which take the sales meeting to each of the regions rather than bring everyone to one place. These programs can be very impressive as the president and other top executives lead off the program with short speeches followed by elaborate presentations given by each of the division directors. How really worthwhile these yearly rituals are is open to question but most companies evidently believe that they are necessary in order to stimulate the selling effort and set goals for the year.

The job of preparing and carrying out these sales programs rests with each of the sales divisions which have the following special responsibilities:

Passenger Sales Division: Responsible for planning and carrying out the sales programs designed to attract new customers and keep regular patrons returning to the airline.

Freight Sales Division: Same as above, but for freight.

Mail Division: Responsible for all contacts with post office department officials. The director works with the airline's schedule division to plan flights which will leave major cities at times which will best fit into the post office department's schedules, thus ensuring large mail loads.

Reservations and Ticket Office Division: Responsible for overseeing the operation of all reservations and ticket offices, planning and opening new offices, training new employees, and surveying the efficiency of the operation from time to time.

Interline Sales Division: Responsible for keeping in touch with sales departments of other airlines to solve mutual problems, encourage cooperation between the carriers, and route as many passengers as possible on each other's planes.

Agency Sales Division: Responsible for planning programs which will increase the interest and cooperation of travel agencies to book more business with the airline.

Convention Sales Division: Responsible for contacting and working with all organizations which will be holding national or regional conventions in cities served by the airline, with the aim of persuading the convention delegates to use the airline. The division provides special services to convention planners and sometimes at the convention itself, such as setting up a special reservations and ticket desk, giving free newspapers to the delegates, opening a delegates' hospitality lounge, and providing transportation to and from the airport for convention officials.

Tariff Division: Responsible for preparing and publishing in company handbooks and timetables all passenger and freight tariffs (fares) between all points served by the airline. Inasmuch as there are all types of promotional and excursion fares this can be an extremely complicated and confusing process.

Market Research Division: Responsible for making surveys of the market for passenger and freight sales. Passenger surveys seek a wide variety of information about passengers which includes statistics on their age, size of family, where they live, income, how frequently they fly, where they fly, time of day they like to depart, where they buy their tickets, how they would like the service improved, and other data which gives a well-rounded picture of the passengers and their preferences. The results can then be used for planning schedules, improving in-flight services (including menus and beverages), improving passenger handling at airports, making changes in reservations and ticketing procedures, and planning advertising and public relations programs. Surveys of air freight shippers obtain pertinent information as it applies to selling and handling air freight.

This division may employ statisticians, stenographers, clerks, and typists in addition to market researchers who should have a Bachelor's degree in marketing and preferably a Master's of Business Administration degree. Trainees often start as junior analysts or research assistants and as they gain experience move up to supervisory positions. Top posts are marketing research director and later vice president for marketing and sales.

Schedule Division: Responsible for preparing all schedules by which the aircraft will operate. This is undoubtedly one of the most difficult but fascinating jobs in the airline. It has been said that a good manager of schedules can make or break a company because there is an art in planning schedules to attract the greatest amount of business and at the same time make use of the aircraft as efficiently as possible.

Lack of space prevents our going into detail about schedule planning, however, we can consider some of the basic factors the schedule section must consider as it draws up the overall system flight pattern.

1. Ideally every city airport manager likes to have flights leave early in the morning for every other important city and return at night so business people can leave and return the same day.
2. Ideally every city manager wants a five o'clock afternoon departure for every other important city.
3. In scheduling transcontinental flights from the west to the east, the three hour time difference presents problems because 3:00 p.m. is the latest time most travelers will take a plane from the west coast to arrive on the east coast at 11:00 p.m. Transcontinental passengers have a preference for a 9:00 a.m. departure from the west and a 5:00 p.m. departure from the east.

4. Adequate provision must be made for "turn-around time"—the time it takes to clean, provision, and check an arriving airplane before it is ready to start its next flight.

5. In busy cities like New York, Chicago, Dallas/Fort Worth, and Atlanta it is important to plan schedules which will provide as many good connections between flights as possible.

6. Each airplane must be scheduled for certain line maintenance work every so many flight hours. This means that it receives servicing and checking by the maintenance department, work which can be performed only at those cities which have the required personnel and equipment. In addition, every aircraft must be taken out of service periodically for a complete overhaul and check at the company's principal maintenance base. This means that each airline always has some airplanes out of service.

7. The flight department must be consulted in preparing schedules because it is responsible for providing the crews (pilots, flight engineers, stewards and stewardesses), but flight personnel are not based in every city. Therefore a flight may have to originate and terminate at a city where crews are based. Furthermore, crews can work only a certain number of hours each day and each month, hence there must be close coordination between schedule planning, aircraft routing, and crew planning specialists.

8. Ultimately the schedule division must be sure that it does not schedule more flights into an airport than can be accommodated at one time.

Little wonder that twice a year when summer and winter schedules are drawn up, the schedule committee (which consists of representatives from various departments) may meet away from the office in a hotel where the members will not be interrupted as they plot the intricate web of scheduling for the coming six months.

Most sales divisions employ numerous assistants or specialists. For example, the tariff division requires economists, statisticians, and statistical clerk/typists. Since the ultimate purpose of all activities carried out by this department is to sell space, anyone interested

The information/reservations department handles calls from travel agents, corporations and other institutions, and individual travelers. Photo: Delta Air Lines.

in a sales career must have a belief in the importance of the sales effort. Throughout the department there will be opportunities for clerical personnel, typists, and stenographers, as well as college-trained men and women who have taken courses in air transportation, sales techniques, and psychology.

For most sales positions a knowledge of airline operation is desirable, if not essential. This is especially true of the schedule division where you may find some specialization: one employee is responsible for all schedules east of Chicago, another for between Chicago and the West schedules, another for utilization of DC-10 equipment, a fourth for all Boeing aircraft, and a fifth for preparing the voluminous timetables and seeing them through the various printing stages to publication and distribution.

This is an age of specialization and this is true in airlines too. If you seek a sales position, find out first what jobs are available. If there are no openings for which you qualify, see if you can begin your career in a reservations or ticket office to get yourself into the company and start gaining experience. Once on the payroll keep your eyes and ears open and let your supervisor know of your interest in working eventually in the sales administrative offices or in the field as a sales representative. In every company there are retirements, resignations, deaths, and dismissals which make opportunities for newcomers like you. Because of its size, an airline sales department is bound to have numerous job openings throughout the system with surprising regularity. If you have prepared yourself, and made your interest known, you should not have difficulty moving into the area that interests you.

Customer service agents greet passengers at the gate and issue boarding passes for flights. Photo: United Airlines.

CHAPTER 6

WORKING WITH CUSTOMERS

The most important thing an airline has to sell is service. Everyone who comes in contact with the customers must be "service oriented" and help make her or his airline known for its careful and courteous treatment of its passengers and shippers. Literally thousands of airline employees have contact in one way or another with the public. They range from the reservations clerk with whom a passenger may make initial contact, to the ticket agent, the passenger service representative, the flight service attendant (the stewardess or steward), and many other employees who work with the public day in and day out. In this chapter we will discuss positions in which you would have opportunity for person-to-person customer relations.

PASSENGER SERVICE REPRESENTATIVE

An advertisement for a major airline featured the picture of a smiling woman dressed in an official airline uniform saying: "I spend all day in the airport so our passengers won't have to." Her job, like that of other passenger service representatives, is to help people.

As passengers stream into a busy terminal they may become confused at the number of people crowded about the ticket counter. A skilled passenger service representative can quickly resolve the problem by seeing to it that people form lines in front of the various agents on duty and that as additional passengers arrive they are taken to the shortest line. Or perhaps in the throng there is a passenger who has little time to make a flight and begins to panic. The alert passenger service representative perceives something is wrong and immediately offers assistance. In no time the passenger is ticketed and on the way to the departure gate.

You will find passenger service representatives wherever there are large numbers of passengers, be it at a ticket counter, reservations office, terminal check-in desk, departure lounge, or sometimes even at the baggage claim area. These individuals are responsible for seeing that everything is functioning smoothly, and that passengers' needs are cared for promptly. They are the company representatives to whom all questions and problems may be referred. In most airlines these employees wear distinctive uniforms or jackets so that they are easily identified.

Passenger service representatives have probably had prior experience working as reservations and/or ticket agents or perhaps as flight attendants. This gives them the necessary background for dealing with most of the problems which arise.

Mention should also be made of the attendants at the airport who work in the departure lounge, the area where passengers wait prior to stepping aboard their flight. The employees who are stationed here to check tickets, assign seats and prepare boarding passes,* may be called flight service representatives or attendants, or they may be passenger service representatives. Whatever their titles, they have responsibilities similar to passenger service representatives except that they work in a more limited area with a group of passengers, all of whom are boarding the same aircraft. Their duties may include helping the flight attendants if there is confusion about a seat assignment or the validity of a boarding pass, and they may have other duties relating to the airplane's departure. This can be one of the more hectic and stressful work areas in an airline. This is especially true if the airplane is not available for boarding at flight time, or if the flight is overbooked and some passengers cannot claim their reservations.

---

*Some airlines assign seats and give passengers their boarding passes when they pick up their tickets.

RESERVATIONS AGENT

Passenger Reservations

Picture yourself seated at a desk in a small cubicle in front of a computer terminal which looks like a typewriter keyboard. At your right is a copy of the latest airline flight schedule book. You are wearing a featherweight telephone headset which leaves both hands free. As customers dial your airline's reservation number, the calls are automatically switched to an agent whose phone is not busy. When all phones are in use a recording tells callers that they will be connected to the first available agent. One measure of good service is the average length of time it takes to answer an incoming call. Airlines are eager to have each call answered just as quickly as possible but naturally do not want to overstaff the reservations office. Hence it is certain that as a reservations agent you will be talking with customers practically all of the time. If you are seeking variety in a desk job, this is it. Probably no two people will make the same requests. Your first caller may want a reservation from Chicago to Detroit and it will take but a minute to handle the call. The next may want you to set up a complicated trip from Chicago to New Orleans, and on to Phoenix, Los Angeles, Spokane, and back to Chicago. This involves several airlines, various fares, dates, and connections. It may take you ten minutes or more to work out the itinerary or you may offer to call the customer back after you have the routing all set.

A survey of all major airlines revealed that the average time for each reservation varied from a low of one minute to a maximum of six, statistics which tell you that a reservations agent handles a lot of calls within an hour. This demands an alert mind and a temperament that can stand dealing with a never-ending succession of phone calls, each requiring individualized treatment and service.

Airlines have installed a variety of reservations systems which use computers of one kind or another. The computers have powerful memories which permit them to perform incredible feats. It is possible to program the computer to keep track of all seats for each flight on every day of the month for months in advance. Thus when an agent has a request for a seat all he or she does is "ask" the computer if one is available and it answers immediately.

At one time airlines maintained a reservations office in each city to handle the business for that area. With the advent of more sophisticated telephone equipment and the expansion of long distance lines, it is now possible to centralize reservations functions so that one office may service all reservations calls coming into a dozen or so cities. This means that you, as a reservations agent, are talking with people from a wide geographical area and the job is made that much more interesting—and complex.

Assume for a moment that you are a "Res Agent" as the job is known in the business. The light on the wall blinks and you flip a switch to answer the incoming call.

"Suburban Airlines, Agent Perez speaking. May I help you?"

"Yes, I want to make two reservations to Washington, D.C., next Tuesday."

"Which airport is most convenient to you and what time would you prefer to leave?"

"Bradley Airport, in Hartford—let's see—sometime in the afternoon."

You make a note on your pad as your fingers fly through the airline guide to the Hartford, Connecticut page.*

"We have flights leaving at two o'clock and four-thirty. Which would you prefer?"

"The two o'clock, please," your customer replies, and immediately you "ask" the computer for two seats by typing your request and giving the date, and airline codes for Hartford and Washington. Thus you might type: HTF-DCA 5/15 Flt 95 2PM 2 sts. You barely finish typing and a green light flashes to indicate the space is available.

"I can confirm the reservation. May I have your name and telephone number, please?"

As the caller dictates the information you type it and thus place this data in the computer. The telephone number is requested in case

---

*Instead of using a printed guide, your airline may enable you to display the information on a small screen beside or above your keyboard.

it is necessary to reach the passenger should the flight be canceled.

You find the fare printed next to the schedule. "The fare will be seventy-five dollars and sixty cents, and you may pick up your tickets any time before the fifteenth. May I make a return reservation?"

"No, thank you, I don't know when we'll be returning."

"Fine, may I suggest you just call our ticket office in Washington when you know your plans. Thank you for calling Suburban and have a good trip."

That call took just two minutes—and now your light is blinking again.

Freight Reservations

Many airlines also employ freight reservations agents who handle requests for cargo space over the phone, quote rates, and answer questions. This job involves not only working with airline schedules but also cargo rates which are more complicated than passenger fares because all types of freight are not charged the same rates. Perishable goods may cost more than nonperishable freight. Priority freight which is loaded first, carries a higher rate than regular cargo. Weight and size also affect rates, as is apparent if you consider that a pound of feathers would take much more space than a pound of lead. The distance a shipment is to be flown also must be taken into account when computing freight rates. All these factors, plus deciding which classification applies to each shipment, call for employees who are alert, imaginative, and able to work with figures.

TICKET AGENT

Ticket agents work in ticket offices located in downtown or suburban locations, often called "city ticket offices," to distinguish them from the airport ticket offices. Ticket agents who work behind a ticket counter make reservations, answer questions about schedules and fares, and prepare ticket forms by writing in the flight number, departure time, passenger's name, destination, and other information. Gradually the computer is taking over much of this ticketing work but the agent still has to instruct the computer how the ticket is to be prepared. In airport offices and some city ticket offices too, an agent also takes the passenger's baggage, weighs it, puts baggage tags on each piece, and places them on a moving belt which takes the luggage to a baggage room.

PASSENGER AGENT

Usually the next step up the ladder for reservations and ticket agents is the position of passenger agent. Passenger agents work only at airports and perform a variety of duties which include helping ticket agents give information, preparing tickets when there is a rush of business, checking baggage, collecting tickets at the gate or departure lounge, assigning seats on a flight, keeping records of passengers boarding a plane, assisting customers who have lost baggage or find their baggage has been damaged, and using the public address system to tell passengers when and where to board as well as to page individual passengers.

During holiday periods or whenever there is bad weather and flights are delayed or canceled, the work can become hectic due to the large number of passengers who crowd the airport, many of whom may want to change their travel plans or request special favors.

One of the best ways to start your airline career is to obtain a position as a reservations or ticket agent. In this post you gain valuable experience in dealing with the customers, planning trips, and selling the service, as well as learning the route structure not only of your own company but of your competitors as well. This knowledge will equip you to undertake many types of work within the company. Many airline executives began their careers on the telephone or behind the ticket counter learning the business from the bottom up.

Airlines are extremely careful about the people they consider hiring as reservations and ticket agents because these employees spend all their time working with the public, and to the customer they are the company. A neat appearance, a pleasing personality, and a good speaking voice are essential, while a high school education is a must and some college training desirable.

If you start your airline career as a reservations or ticket agent you will probably spend a training period in a classroom learning how to use the flight schedule directory, compute fares, and work with the computer. You will also be taught how to handle and talk with customers courteously and efficiently. Then you will receive two or three weeks on-the-job training as you work with experienced employees, and finally you will be on your own but performing your duties under the watchful eye and careful direction of a knowledgeable supervisor.

Advancement is limited for most agents but if you are ambitious you may move up to become a passenger agent, then passenger service representative, or perhaps a supervisor. Eventually you might win promotion to the position of airport or city ticket office manager and, if you have aptitude at selling, to district sales manager. Opportunities for promotion are not limited to these posts, however, but the important thing is to get your start, demonstrate what you can and want to do, and watch for any unusual openings for which you qualify.

FREIGHT AGENT

Air freight is a growing part of almost every airline's business. Many companies fly hugh air freighters in addition to carrying freight in the cargo compartments of their passenger aircraft. As trucks draw up to an airport freight depot, freight agents are on hand to carry out a variety of jobs such as loading and unloading freight from trucks and airplanes, preparing shipping documents, providing information, storing and checking freight kept in storage, tying down freight in aircraft, preparing freight manifests, handling complaints regarding late, lost, or damaged freight, and keeping company freight records.

If this end of the business interests you and you are hired to work at the airport, you will probably start learning the business by doing manual labor and later be given responsibility for preparing shipping documents and manifests and working in the office. This is a busy part of the company and there is opportunity to gain promotion to other positions once you have proven your ability to handle bigger assignments than may be available in the air freight area.

FLIGHT ATTENDANT

A cheerful woman in a fashionable tailored blue uniform, Geri Miller stood just inside the first class cabin to greet the passengers.

"May I see your boarding pass?" she asked each passenger as he or she approached. She quickly directed each to the first class seats or to the coach section in the rear. As soon as most of the passengers were on board she started hanging up the coats of the first class passengers, noting the seat numbers on special tags which she attached to the garments. Having completed this, she picked up a pile of evening newspapers and walked up the aisle, offering copies to passengers in the first class cabin and also verifying the name of each passenger on the seating diagram. The diagram is then hung in the galley and enables the attendants to address each passenger by her or his last name. By the time she had given out the last paper, Geri heard the passenger service attendant close the main door. A moment later the plane was being towed by a tractor and was quietly moving away from the loading gate.

She went quickly up the aisle checking each row of passengers to make certain seat belts were fastened and there were no large boxes, suitcases, or other objects in empty seats or on the floor. Safety rules require that during takeoff or landing nothing be left in the way of passengers who might have to leave the airplane suddenly in event of an emergency.

"Please fasten your seat belt and observe the 'No Smoking' sign," she said pleasantly to a smoker who was engrossed in reading a novel.

"That dispatch box will have to go under your seat during takeoff, Mr. Lasko," she told another passenger whose name she remembered. "And then will you please fasten your seat belt?"

Meanwhile her partner, Pat Mahler, had turned on the public address system and was welcoming the passengers. Geri then stood in the front of the cabin and held up an oxygen mask. As Pat read the required instructions regarding the use of the mask, Geri demonstrated how to use the oxygen masks should the cabin suddenly lose its pressurization.

". . . a mask will automatically drop before you. Bring the mask to your face, breathe deeply . . . " Pat read as Geri showed what to do.

As the attendants finished their demonstration the plane paused at the end of the runway and the crew departed for their takeoff. Geri gave the galley a last minute check to make certain nothing was loose and then took her seat opposite the galley seconds before the captain released the brakes and applied full power.

As Geri sat next to Pat she kicked off her shoes. Her feet were tired from the incoming flight she had just worked from Louisville to Boston. Now she was enroute back to Chicago, her second flight for the day. She thought back to when she had applied for the job. It all seemed so romantic, so glamorous. She had not known about the need to check the cabin before each flight, the continuous and tiring demands made on one during a flight, especially a short one, the irregular hours and assignments, or the aching feet! She smiled, thinking of all that had happened since she agreed to become a flight attendant. It had been hard work and much time away from home, but it had been satisfying and she wouldn't have missed it for anything!

Now as the plane lifted and she heard the familiar sound of the wheels being retracted, she wiggled on her shoes and got to her feet. There was a lot to do and not much time. She and Pat had worked together before and they functioned as a smooth team. Actually, their training had been so thorough that even when attendants worked together for the first time, they knew exactly what each should do and how to divide the work. Today there were twenty-eight passengers to be served drinks and a full-course dinner—all within an hour and ten minutes. Flight time was approximately an hour and a half, but ten minutes had to be allowed for both takeoff and landing.

The two attendants opened the doors of the buffet, took out napkins, silverware, and all the other items which had been packed there by the commissary department. Pat set up the beverage cart. Geri removed bottles from their cases and five minutes later they were moving up the aisle, setting up trays in front of each passenger, and serving drinks, Pat on the left side, Geri on the right.

The attendants pushed their cart back to the galley as soon as the last drink was served and started assembling the dinners. The various courses came packed in specially refrigerated boxes and heated ovens so that it was only necessary to take the fruit cup from one box, the complete dinner from a warming oven, and the salad, butter, and dessert from another box. Napkins, utensils, salt and pepper, and a coffee cup completed the setting for each tray. Once the last tray was out, Geri appeared with a silver coffee pot while Pat began to pack away the used beverage glasses. Suddenly the captain buzzed. Pat went immediately to the cockpit door and looked in.

"How about a cup of coffee for the workers on this flight?" the captain asked. "Be some time before we get dinner."

"Same with me," Pat said as she smiled, "but I can get some for you." Nothing was too much trouble when the crew asked for something.

"Time to clean up," Geri said as she glanced at her watch and once more they were in the aisle, this time removing the trays and then stacking them in the galley. Geri could sense the airplane start its descent and feel the speed decrease as the crew cut back the power.

"Ladies and gentlemen," the captain said on the intercom, "we have started our descent into the O'Hare Airport area and will be landing in fifteen minutes. We hope you have had a pleasant flight. Thank you for flying with us, and we look forward to serving you again."

Now the attendants worked rapidly to get everything put away. Pat concentrated on cleaning up the galley while Geri checked the cabin to make certain all trays were folded and stored and that all briefcases were under the seats. There was a gentle chime and the seat belt sign flashed on, which meant a second check to make certain everyone had their belts secured. Then the airplane took a wide swing and the wheels could be heard lowering and locking into place. Another chime signaled that the captain had turned on the "No Smoking" sign. A final quick walk up and down the aisle to make sure there were no offenders. Then as the plane rushed toward the ground Geri took her seat in time to fasten her seat belt before the wheels touched the ground. A moment later when the plane was taxiing slowly to its gate, the two attendants were up again to get coats out of the closet and hand them back to their owners before the plane pulled up to the gate at the terminal and passengers could disembark.

Just as people say goodnight to departing guests, the attendants say good-bye to passengers who have been their guests on the flight.

"Good night, good night, thank you, nice to have had you aboard, good night, good night . . . ," and at last the passengers are gone.

Now to write up the flight report which records any irregularities or problems the maintenance crew should fix, and a few minutes later the flight attendants were hurrying through the terminal toward the platform where the bus left for Chicago's Loop. Geri and Pat would room in one of the hotels and at noon the next day each would leave Chicago on different planes.

This Boston-Chicago flight was not typical because there is no such thing as a typical flight. While Geri and Pat served the twenty-eight first class passengers, three other flight attendants were equally pressed for time to feed a hundred and forty passengers in the coach section. On the other hand, if an attendant is working a five-hour transcontinental flight, there may be time to sit down and relax, plus there are many shorter flights on which no meals are served, but only beverages and snacks. On the whole, however, an attendant can count on being busy unless there are few passengers on board.[3]

Speaking of changed working conditions for flight attendants, Bev Nelson, an attendant for Western Airlines who had twenty-five years seniority, said:

"A lot of things have changed. The training's far better of course. When I got out of McDonnell training school, you didn't need any more training—you just rode with another attendant on each type of airplane Western was operating, and you learned on the job—usually by trial and error, fun but not very efficient. Passengers have changed, too. When I started, they got a little white cake box with bologna sandwiches and bread that curled up at the ends. Plus a carton of milk. Everyone thought that was really living. Now they're all gourmets. They ask what kind of red wine it is, or what brand of scotch you are offering, or if it is a filet mignon or New York cut steak.

---

[3]Many of the airlines which offer cut-rate fares do not serve meals and may offer only coffee or cold drinks and snacks.

Flight attendants respond to individual passenger needs during flights, serving beverages and food. Photo: Delta Air Lines.

"Flight crews used to be a lot closer. Now I see captains I've never met. And the new attendants are different. When I began flying, you had to fight for your job—the airlines were hiring one attendant at a time. You had to wait until somebody resigned or was terminated before you could get on. In some ways, the job was tougher. I remember bidding a trip that had thirteen stops between Los Angeles and Minneapolis.

"Galleys are better, although I suppose there will never be a galley that's completely satisfactory to an attendant."

Airlines stress the proper training of their flight attendants and go to great lengths and expense to provide the best instruction. This is because of all employees on the payroll, flight attendants spend the most time with passengers and are directly responsible for the comfort of every person on board, as well as for their safety in the event of an emergency.

If you are accepted as a flight attendant trainee you will find that many airlines have their own training schools where you stay for several weeks of intensive instruction in specific subjects such as routes, schedules, flight regulations, first aid, emergency procedures and evacuation, good grooming, and etiquette.

Just before completing your training you will take practice flights as an observer and possibly be permitted to assist experienced attendants with some of their work. After graduation you will be assigned to a main crew base and at first may fill in on extra flights or take the place of attendants who are sick or on vacation. Assignments are made on the basis of seniority so that experienced attendants can have their choice of flights and times.

Advancement is limited. You might later transfer to a position as flight service instructor in the training school, as customer service representative, or possibly as recruiting representative in the personnel department.

An increasing number of women are rising through airline ranks to work as flight officers. Photo: American Airlines.

CHAPTER 7

THE FLIGHT CREW

At the end of the runway of the San Francisco airport the Boeing 707 stood poised, its crew awaiting permission from the control tower to take off. Captain Thomas Rawlins, a gray-haired veteran, was in the front left seat of the cockpit and at his right sat the younger First Officer, Juan Benez. Behind Benez Flight Engineer Arnold Mitchell was at his flight engineer's panel, his experienced eyes expertly checking the numerous lights, dials, and gauges which told him the exact conditions existing in the engines, the rate of fuel flow, and other important data about the airplane and its intricate mechanisms. He noted that the indicators showed the brakes were now locked, the flaps were down—in fact, everything was in order.

"Flight 76 cleared for takeoff," the voice of the controller in the tower crackled from the loud speaker.

"Full forward on the wheel," Captain Rawlins said gently, and the first officer pushed the yoke of the control column forward. As he did so a control surface far back at the rear of the plane gradually moved, its function being to keep the nose of the plane down during the takeoff. Meanwhile Captain Rawlins grasped the control wheel which steered the two wheels up front in the nose gear, and at the same time moved the pedals to release the brakes.

There was a slight shudder and, free of the restraining brakes, the huge airliner was ready to respond to the power packed in each of the whining engines. Rolling forward easily, the plane gradually accelerated. The ground slipped by faster and faster, yellow marker lights rushed by, and it seemed nothing on earth could stop the plane.

"One hundred knots," Benez said. Then seconds later: "One hundred thirty-six knots," and the aircraft was airborne. Captain Rawlins released the steering wheel and his feet again pushed the rudder pedals to control the plane's direction.

"V one," First Officer Benez announced tensely. "V one" is the speed at which the airplane can proceed or stop, actually the point of no return. If something goes wrong and the plane must remain on the ground, this is the maximum speed to which it can be accelerated and still be brought to a safe stop on the runway—assuming there is sufficient pavement left if this should be necessary. At "V one" the airplane was moving at about 145 knots or 167 miles an hour.

"Rotate." Benez said, and the captain pulled back on the yoke to change the position of the elevators slightly, thus forcing the tail down a bit and enabling the plane to climb at a greater angle. Now they were approaching "V two." 162 knots or 187 miles per hour, climbing rapidly with the speed steadily increasing.

"Up gear," Rawlins commanded, and with his left hand the first officer pulled a lever to make the ten-wheeled landing gear retract into its wells. Immediately metal doors snapped shut to encase all the wheels, and the plane was groomed for its flight.

Two hundred knots and "Up flaps!" Benez touched the proper control and the flaps moved into position with their outboard ailerons locked in place. The speakers overhead came to life as a voice from Air Traffic Control announced: "Cleared to 12,000 feet."

Now there was the sound of gently hissing air rushing by the fuselage and Flight 76 was on its way. First Officer Benez snapped off the "No Smoking" signs in the cabin as the attendants rose from their seats and prepared to serve beverages. Meanwhile the passengers, who would soon be cruising eight miles about the earth's surface, relaxed in anticipation of an enjoyable transcontinental flight.

Captain Rawlins reached for the microphone and flipped the switch which connected him with all the speakers throughout the cabin.

"Good morning, ladies and gentlemen, this is Captain Rawlins speaking on behalf of your crew, First Officer Benez and Flight Engineer Mitchell. Welcome aboard, and we hope you have a very pleasant flight. Today our flight plan will take us over Denver, Colorado;

Wichita, Kansas; St. Louis, Missouri; and Erie, Pennsylvania. Our speed will average about 659 miles an hour, our cruising altitude will be 40,000 feet, and we anticipate a smooth flight. Thank you."

Now, while the airplane rushes along at more than ten miles a minute, let us examine the duties of the flight crew in a bit more detail.

DUTIES OF AN AIRPLANE PILOT

Pilots are skilled, highly trained professionals. Although many pilots work for airlines flying passengers, cargo, and mail, there are others who fly for private companies or perform tasks such as taking photographs, inspecting power lines, or crop dusting.

Two pilots are usually required to fly each plane, except on small aircraft. Usually the most experienced pilot, who is called the captain by the airlines, is in command of the plane and supervises all other crew members on board. The copilot generally helps in communicating with the air traffic controllers, monitoring the flight instruments, and flying the plane. If the captain were unable to perform efficiently for any reason, the copilot would be in charge. Most large planes have a third pilot in the cockpit who serves as the flight engineer. It is the flight engineer's duty, as we have noted, to monitor and operate many of the instruments, and also make minor in-flight repairs and watch out for other aircraft.

The pilots work together an hour or more before departure to plan their flight, conferring with weather forecasters and dispatchers to learn all they can about weather conditions both en route and at their destination. Having all this information at hand, they plot their route, altitude, and the speed which will give a fast, safe, and smooth flight. It is also becoming increasingly important to plan a flight so as to use as little fuel as possible, but this is never as important a consideration as safety and comfort. Once the flight has been planned the pilot in command of the airplane must inform Air Traffic Control about the flight plan so that it can be coordinated with all of the other traffic.

Another preflight duty for the pilots is thoroughly to check their aircraft to make certain that all controls, engines, instruments, and other components are in good working order. They also are concerned to know that mail, baggage, and cargo have all been loaded correctly.

Most difficult and sometimes dangerous parts of the flight are the takeoff and landing, which require the closest possible coordination between a pilot and copilot. While the plane is accelerating for take-off, the pilot concentrates on watching the runway while the copilot watches the instrument panel. They know the speed which must be attained in order to be airborne, having taken into account the altitude of the airport, the weight of the airplane, and the direction and speed of the wind. The instant the plane reaches this critical speed the copilot informs the pilot who actuates the control to raise the nose of the aircraft.

The work may be routine and easy, once airborne and at cruising altitude, especially if weather conditions are favorable. From time to time it is necessary to radio air speed, position, and other details to the nearest air traffic control station. The pilots continuously scan their instrument panels to make certain the engines are functioning correctly. Occasionally they may request air traffic control to permit a change of altitude in order to have a smoother or swifter flight by taking advantage of tailwinds which help save fuel.

When visibility is poor, the pilots must rely on instruments. Thanks to the altimeter they know how far above the ground they are flying and they can maneuver around high mountains or other obstacles. It is possible for them to compute their exact position by using a special navigation radio and maps. Other sophisticated radio equipment will guide a pilot to the end of a runway for a "blind" landing when weather conditions are such that the ground cannot be seen from the air.

The flight engineer is a trouble-shooter, monitor, and backup for the pilots. Before flight time the engineer walks about the aircraft checking approximately 200 items. He or she oversees fueling operations, reviews mechanics' reports, and helps the captain make the preflight cockpit check. During the flight, the engineer monitors the engines, keeps track of fuel consumption, and the heating, pressurization, hydraulic, electrical, and air-conditioning systems, and may also repair faulty equipment. The flight engineer must also check and maintain aircraft log books, report mechanical difficulties to mechanic crew chiefs, and at the end of the trip make a final postflight inspection of the airplane.

Before we consider the educational and physical requirements for these jobs, let's rejoin Flight 76 and its crew. On this particular day the eastern part of the United States was enjoying unusually fine weather with excellent visibility, and therefore no landing delays were anticipated.

THE LANDING

As the flight neared Erie, Pennsylvania, Captain Rawlins swung the plane about slightly and headed for Allentown. Once the 707 was over Allentown, Kennedy International Airport was only ninety miles to the east and the captain commenced his descent. The aircraft was going more slowly, 465 miles an hour, and dropping an average of 2,500 feet a minute.

Now the crew was busy! First Officer Benez was in constant radio communication with the Kennedy Approach Control, receiving his instructions for the final approach to the airport. The New York metropolitan air space is one of the busiest in the United States and therefore the crew members would be watching for any other planes that might threaten a mid-air collision.

Flight Engineer Mitchell was studying his panel carefully. Among other tasks he saw to it that the cabin pressure dropped in accordance with their descent. He leaned over to adjust the cabin pressure control, making the barometric correction equal to the same elevation above Kennedy Airport.

The three flight crew members were going through their prelanding checklists as they checked their flight instruments, controls, lights, pressures, and various dials. At the same time the airplane had become an active light blip on the Kennedy radarscope in the control tower thirty miles away.

"Flaps at thirty degrees," the captain ordered, and the first officer moved the flap handle until it was at the thirty degree position. Soon an indicator confirmed that this had taken place. "Flaps thirty degrees," Benez informed the captain. As these large sections of the wings slid back and downward they changed the airflow of the plane and made it easier to control the landing.

Once the air speed was down to 200 miles per hour the captain ordered "Gear down." and the first officer pushed the appropriate lever. Immediately the doors under the fuselage opened and the plane experienced a distinct rumble as air rushed over the open wells. Six seconds later the nose gear was down and locked into place, and four seconds after that the ten-wheeled main gear was down. The captain knew that it had been secured by the bright green light that appeared on the instrument panel.

By now the plane was flying parallel to the runway on which it was scheduled to land, but in the opposite direction to the planned landing. Air speed was now 180 miles per hour, and the right wing went down as Captain Rawlins turned the airliner about for its descent. At this altitude of a thousand feet another bank of the plane straightened it out readying it for the drop to its final landing. The first officer called out the rate that the airplane was descending ("sink rate").

"Full flaps." Captain Rawlins commanded, and First Officer Benez pulled back the flap handle as far as it would go and locked it into place. Suddenly the end of the runway disappeared below and the airspeed registered 160 miles. Carefully the captain nudged the control yoke back so that the plane was sinking at the rate of approximately seven feet a second, and then the wheels gently reached the pavement.

The instant the main gear wheels touched the concrete the captain pushed the yoke forward causing the nose to dip and easing the nose wheels to the ground. As these wheels met the ground the captain pulled the speed brake handle and on each wing a "spoiler" raised up some sixty degrees causing a sudden drag which helped slow the heavy airplane.

More than spoilers was needed to check the speed of 151 miles per hour, however. Just in front of the throttle knobs, on the same shaft of each, are "reverse thrust levers." When the captain grasped and pulled these up and then back, there was an immediate reaction within each engine. Clamshell doors quickly closed, effectively blocking the engines' tail pipes and making the jet exhaust go forward. Then, as the captain speeded up the engines, the plane began to slow down and he again steered the craft with the nose wheels, soon turning off the main runway to taxi to the terminal.

The flight engineer had been busy watching his instrument panel for signs of any possible malfunctioning. Now he was busy shutting off the anti-icing devices, turning off the heat for the cockpit windows, extinguishing the emergency exit lights in the cabin, and cutting off power in the galleys, as well as flipping countless other switches.

At the terminal the airplane swung about, the captain locked the brakes, and shut down the first three engines but left number four on to provide power for the electrical system. As soon as the ground personnel arrived and plugged in the power cables Rawlins shut off the fourth engine, and the airplane became suddenly quiet. Passengers stood up, put on their coats, and waited for the cabin door to be opened so that they could leave. Flight 76 had become just another statistic—but on the apron below, the cleaning and maintenance crews were waiting to ready the plane for a flight to Houston.

The flight crew members were the last to leave the plane, and as they walked through the crowded terminal, dressed in their trim brown uniforms, they could not help but notice the many admiring glances cast at them. The public still looks upon the pilot's job as an exciting and glamorous one, but few people appreciate the responsibility which falls directly on the shoulders of a professional flight crew, headed by one individual, the captain. Nor are many aware of the stringent physical health demands made on those who fly our nation's transport planes—so demanding in fact, that every pilot must pass a thorough physical examination every six months or be grounded. Actually, when you consider the necessary qualifications for this job, you will see why pilots are among the highest paid employees in any airline.

BASIC REQUIREMENTS

The Air Line Pilots Association has this to say about the physical requirements and education of a commercial airline pilot:

No other career requires physical health demands as stringent as those in flying, especially those of an air transport pilot and a business pilot with an air transport pilot's license. It is strongly urged that *before* beginning pilot training, aspirants obtain a first-class medical certificate from a local FAA medical examiner. Acquisition and maintenance of this certificate is the key to earning a living in flying. Most airlines require an uncorrected distance visual acuity of 20/20 or better in each eye. However, some airlines do allow vision correctable to 20/20 or better in each eye with corrective lenses—glasses or contact lenses.

The commercial airline pilot profession is a highly skilled and technical one demanding a high degree of mental dexterity. The airline pilot works with technically complex avionic systems, must possess the ability to think clearly in times of stress and be able to make split-second decisions based on sound judgment. He or she must have a thorough grasp of mathematics, aerodynamics, aeronautics and navigation.

Acquisition of these skills begins at the secondary level of education with an emphasis on the basic sciences, particularly mathematics and physics. At the college or university level, studies in aeronautical engineering, advanced mathematics, the sciences and aviation-related courses are excellent preparation for a career as a pilot.

College counselors can provide suggestions and consultation as to the curriculum that should be followed. High school guidance counselors can provide information on scholarships and financial aid.

OPPORTUNITIES FOR TRAINING

There are several ways to acquire pilot training. The first is through flight instruction at flying schools certified by the Federal Aviation Administration. You must be at least 16 years of age and be able to pass a third class medical examination. Courses consist of forty hours of ground school instruction where you learn the principles of flight, aerial navigation, weather factors, and flight regulations. Flying lessons are conducted in dual-controlled aircraft (twenty-five hours dual and ten hours solo instruction). The instructor judges when you are ready to take the written and flight examinations which are given by Federal Aviation Administration inspectors. Upon successful completion of both exams, you earn your private pilot's license which entitles you to fly passengers, but not for hire. As a private pilot you can then undertake advanced instruction, learn to fly on instruments, and earn a commercial pilot's license upon acquiring additional hours of flight experience. These achievements open up numerous pilot careers because now you can fly for hire. Further study and experience could eventually earn you the Air Transport Rating to qualify as an airline pilot.

A second method of acquiring flight training is through pilot training in the armed forces. This entails no personal financial expense and, as a military pilot, you can qualify for numerous civilian pilot jobs upon leaving the service with some additional study. The military services have been a major source of pilots for the airlines in the past.

Third, a growing number of colleges and universities offer flight training with credit toward a degree. As a graduate, you leave school with a private or commercial license, and possibly an Air Transport Rating, plus a degree.

Helicopter pilots can receive training in the armed forces or at special private helicopter flight schools certified by the Federal Aviation Administration.

Agricultural pilots can receive specialized advanced training at agricultural pilot schools.

Some airlines offer training courses for corporate pilots transitioning to new jet aircraft. The airlines' experience in jet flight training makes them particularly well qualified to provide this service to business firms.

Flight crew members inspect the exterior of the aircraft for safe maintenance before takeoff. Photo: American Airlines.

CHAPTER 8

OPERATING SAFELY AND EFFICIENTLY

THE STATION MANAGER

As our bus pulled into Kennedy International Airport, it was dark and snowing. Within the airline terminal we found a passenger service representative, told her we had an eight o'clock appointment with David Ingstrum, the station manager, and asked for directions. Several minutes later, after walking along endless corridors, down twisting stairs, and through more hallways, we were ushered into a large office with a picture window looking out at the ramp. At one side of the room there was a long table with a dozen chairs about it.

A heavyset man dressed in a dark blue suit rose to greet us.

"You surely picked a bad night," Mr. Ingstrum said after we shook hands. He pointed to the snow-covered area outside the building where workers were busy loading baggage into an airplane. "Another two or three inches and we'll be closed—just like Philadelphia." He snapped his fingers. "That reminds me, excuse me a moment." He picked up one of the two telephones on his desk, tapped out a number, and a few seconds later asked: "Everything set for those Philly passengers on Flight 163?" He listened intently, said "Fine, thank you," and put the phone down.

"Flight 163 has forty-seven passengers on board for Philadelphia," he explained, "but that airport's closed, so when the flight arrives here we'll have to take care of them. Thank goodness they've had their dinner so all we have to do is get two buses to take them on to Philadelphia. When airplanes can't make it to their scheduled destination it can be rough on the station that has to receive them—

especially if there's only a manager and a couple of agents on duty. If we close down later tonight I imagine flight dispatch will send the planes to Pittsburgh or Buffalo—they're both open, and I pity those stations!" He paused a second to glance out the window again. "Well, that's not your problem and I gather you want to know what a station manager does, is that right?"

"Correct. Could you first give us some idea of what your overall responsibilities are?"

He laughed. "Everything—actually I'm responsible for all the flight and ground operations here. That includes passenger services, air cargo operations, handling and servicing the airplanes. From the moment the passenger steps off the airport bus or out of the taxi until he or she walks onto the airplane and the aircraft pulls away from the terminal, I'm responsible." He paused a second and smiled. "I forgot—of course, at the other end when the planes arrive—from the time the captain cuts the engines and passengers start to leave the plane, we're responsible for seeing that the customers get their baggage and find their transportation to the city, that the cargo and mail are properly handled, and that the airplane is serviced and made ready for its next trip. Sound impressive?"

"Certainly does—but where do you fit into the organization?" we asked.

Mr. Ingstrum laughed. "A year ago I was under another department, now I'm part of the operations department, but in some airlines I'd report to the city manager instead of to the operations vice president. Airlines are forever changing their organizations but it doesn't really matter. There's a big job to be done and everyone here works hard at it."

"What categories of employees does a station like yours have?" we asked next.

"Office workers—the usual stenographers, typists, and clerks—but not many of them." He bit his lip and looked at the ceiling. "Let's think in terms of entering the terminal," he said. "First there is the Skycap who wheels in the passenger's luggage. That's an important job because often that individual is the first person to welcome an arriving passenger and the initial impression is important. Then, moving into the terminal we have the ticket agents behind the counter, the passenger service agents who also work at counters and in the departure lounges, and the passenger service representatives. Moving out to the airplanes, we have our largest group of employees, the ramp service people—the men and women who service the airplanes at this station." He pointed out the window. "You can see many of them working on that airplane now."

Through the falling snowflakes we could see figures wiping the plane, loading cargo into the lower compartments of the fuselage, and two men up on a wing dragging a hose to refuel the aircraft.

"Everyone who works at this station takes orders from my staff," he continued, "although they may follow procedures drawn up by other departments as do the ticket agents and the maintenance people." He glanced at a memorandum on his desk. "I see you're going from here to the operations office in the hangar. That's entirely separate from us—they serve the whole company—we just operate this station and service the airplanes in the hangar or on the ramp."

We asked Mr. Ingstrum about the ramp personnel. He told us that the term *ramp* is a bit misleading, for one of the definitions the dictionary gives is "a stairway for entering or leaving the main door of an airplane." However, at stations like this, passengers enter and leave aircraft from the second story of the terminal and no outside stairway is used. Thus the term *ramp personnel* has come to mean airline employees who service the inside and outside of a plane or work outdoors in the vicinity of an airplane. They could just as well be called "apron" personnel inasmuch as the apron refers to the paved part of an airport adjacent to a terminal building or hangar. Another term for ramp personnel is fleet service workers, which seems more descriptive of what they do.

When an airplane completes its flight schedule and the cabin is empty, the ramp service people swarm aboard, equipped with vacuum cleaners, brooms, dust cloths, and other cleaning equipment. The floor and seats are vacuumed, trash is picked up, headrests and pillow covers are replaced, blankets refolded and stored, seat packets refilled, lavatories and buffets cleaned, and cockpit windows washed. If the aircraft is returning to service, this work may have to been done quickly and the job finished fifteen to twenty minutes before the first passengers start arriving.

Other ramp service people clean the exterior of the plane, meanwhile, using special brushes, sponges, mops, and hoses to do the work. They may work on scaffolding or in special lift equipment in order to reach higher parts of the airplane. Occasionally one of them may have to touch up the paint if there is a bad scratch or dent. If time permits an airplane may be towed into the hangar where this work is performed, but on a fast turnaround, the job must be done outdoors regardless of the weather conditions. Since most airplanes do not fly at night the heaviest work schedule falls during the night hours.

Baggage and cargo handlers represent another group of ramp service people who load and unload baggage, air mail, air express, and freight shipments. They drive baggage tow-carts, operate fork lifts, conveyors, fork trucks, and other baggage and air freight handling equipment. They may also run the machinery which sorts and routes the baggage and air cargo to and from various flights. These employees work outdoors on noisy crowded aprons in all kinds of weather and must do much lifting, moving, pushing, and positioning of baggage, mail sacks, and cargo.

Aircraft fuelers who operate the fueling equipment drive a fuel truck. First they fill the truck with aviation fuel at the tank farm or fuel storage depot, then they deliver it to the aircraft where they turn on the pumps, pull out the long heavy hose, then climb up onto the wings to reach the fuel tank openings. One must be sure-footed in rainy or snowy weather!

Drivers are also employed to operate food trucks, employee buses, conveyors which lift freight up to the plane, mobile stairs (at airports where passengers do not enter or leave aircraft from the terminal building), cleaning equipment, power carts, and aircraft air-conditioning units. Auto mechanics are needed to keep all of this equipment operating at top efficiency as well as to make emergency repairs.

Ramp service people must have a high school diploma and those who drive should have a driver's license and possibly a chauffeur's license too. Handlers of cargo and baggage should be in good health and have the physical strength needed for lifting and moving heavy bags and boxes.

A worker may start at the low-paying job of cleaner and move up to better paying positions such as driver, aircraft fueler, or baggage handler. Once you have experience at a variety of ramp service positions you may be promoted to a desk job in an administrative position. One of these is ramp planner, whose responsibility it is to keep track of arriving and departing aircraft and to dispatch service units to them—cleaners, fuelers, baggage handlers, and food service trucks.

"The ramp planner can have a hectic time," Mr. Ingstrum added. "Especially on a night like this with extra flights arriving and snow to keep off wings and the automotive equipment."

He glanced at the clock. "You're due over at flight operations at nine. You can just catch the crew car now. It goes every half hour between the terminal here and the hangar. I'll tell the driver it's all right for you to ride."

A few minutes later we were riding in a station wagon over a bumpy road toward the hangar which was a mile and a quarter away. It was evident that the driver had to know the way and be extra alert as we wound over twisting service roads and across strips where airplanes were taxiing to and from the main runways. Visibility was poor with the snow still coming down and we wondered whether the airport would be closed soon. At the hangar the driver led us to the flight operations room and pointed out Albert Watkins, the flight dispatcher, who was talking with two other workers. "I'll tell him you're here—just take a seat and he'll be with you soon."

FLIGHT DISPATCHER

From our end of the busy room we watched as Mr. Watkins conferred with several pilots, walking back and forth from his desk to study weather charts on the wall at one end of the room, then talking briefly with other employees who were working at desks scattered about the room. The noise of the teletype machines chattering, telephones ringing, typewriters clacking, intercom crackling, and conversations sometimes rising above the general hubbub made us wonder how anyone working here could concentrate, but everyone seemed quite used to it.

Mr. Watkins waved to us at last and we went over to his desk and sat down on the side chairs he pulled up for us. "Sorry to keep you waiting," he said, "but I had two flights out at nine to button up. Now I'm off duty and someone else is in charge." He picked up a cup of coffee and took a long drink, leaned back in his chair, and shook his head slowly.

"It's been a hectic day—whenever we have snow it fouls up the schedules, the airports, the loading and unloading. Everything gets behind and then trouble seems to gang up on you. Suddenly you're faced with a series of questions: What's the weather doing to the flights? What's it like out there in Philadelphia, Buffalo, Pittsburgh, Washington, and a score of other cities? What is it like at the destination city for each flight we dispatch? What alternate airports should we consider if it's impossible to land at the destination? How much fuel will be left to get the plane to an alternate airport if necessary?"

He works with the captain of each flight, going over the flight plan, which means they must study the winds aloft, the altitudes at which the flight will cruise, the traffic flow of other planes, the weather at the destination, the expected weight of the plane, the amount of fuel that will be needed, and which airports they should plan to send the airplane to if it is not possible to land at the scheduled destination.

"In addition to doing everything I can to ensure a safe flight," he said, "it's my responsibility to see that the plane gets to its destination on time, with the maximum load possible, but at the least operating cost. That's a big order, especially when you think of all the factors we have to take into consideration and the number of flights we clear out of here." He took another sip of coffee and put the cup down. "I don't know how many times I've signed that release form with the pilot. Oh . . ." he noted the quizzical look on our faces, "of course, no flight can take off until the pilot and flight dispatcher sign the release which indicates we've prepared a flight plan and all is in order."

He pointed to a pile of papers at one corner of his desk. "Those are loading reports—some of the documents we have to consult—they tell us how many passengers and how much weight are expected on board, including the weight of the fuel. We need to know this to compute the mileage we can get as well as the cost of the flight." He paused and smiled. "Sounds mighty complicated I guess, but actually we have these handy calculators and there is always the computer, too, to make it easier."

"In fact the computer is taking on more and more of the work of preparing flight plans, so much so that the way we operate here is now old-fashioned in many ways because in some companies the computer has almost taken over the flight dispatcher's job! I know of one airline where they have stored computerized routes which are all preplanned so that if a pilot is going to fly from Nashville to Chicago, the dispatcher prints out the flight plan on the computer. All this makes the job of the flight dispatcher easier and really less demanding although he still has certain duties." He leaned back and smiled slightly. "Probably none of this is too important to your readers because by the time they apply for the job, everything will have changed again—this is an industry of change."

"It certainly seems so," we agreed. "But tell us how one becomes a flight dispatcher."

"It takes time," he replied. "Most dispatchers move up from jobs as station managers, meteorologists, radio operators, junior flight dispatchers, or dispatch clerks. Actually you must know the Civil Air Regulations and the airline's operations rules and have a Federal Aviation Administration dispatcher's license. I'd say that a college education with a major in meteorology or air transportation would be adequate preparation. In a small airline, the flight dispatcher also has to be a meteorologist and a schedule coordinator too. No one is going to walk in here from school and sit at this desk. I guess that's quite obvious—you have to have a lot of experience—but it's not a bad job. In fact, just think, there are eight or ten flights our there right now which I cleared—makes you feel important in one way, and humble in another." He rose and stretched. "Guess you might say that if you sit at this desk you earn your money!"

Mr. Watkins pointed out Elaine Philips, the schedule coordinator at the other end of the huge operations room. "Elaine's on the phone but she won't mind if we just go on over and wait for her in front of her desk."

SCHEDULE COORDINATOR

"Sit down please, I'll be with you in a sec," Ms. Philips said as she held the phone to her ear. A moment later she put the receiver down. "It's been a rough evening. We had to divert some flights from Philadelphia and one plane which stopped at Philly couldn't get out. Have you any idea what that entails?" We confessed we did not.

"It means that the station manager at Philadelphia has to feed 150 people and then get them to Newark which is their destination."

"But how?" we asked, "especially if the airport is closed?"

"Bus or train. The manager has contacts with the local bus companies and by the time they finish eating in the terminal dining room there'll be four buses lined up outside. But meanwhile the manager's got a couple of hundred passengers who can't get their flights out." She smiled, "I'd rather have this job any time! Now let me tell you what I do!"

Between phone calls she told us her responsibility was to keep track of all the aircraft and crews coming into or leaving the airport. If an airplane is delayed because of weather or a mechanical problem, she informs everyone concerned about the delays and changes in plans. If an airplane has to be taken out of service, it is her job to order a substitute which might mean combining flights or even canceling another flight if no back-up plane is available.

If bad weather affects air traffic, delaying the estimated time a plane will arrive or takeoff, or requiring an unscheduled stop *en route*, it is she who must think it all out and tell everyone who needs to know. When an extra airplane must be made available for a flight, she must first take into consideration what servicing or maintenance requirements may apply to that aircraft. For example, if it is due for line maintenance after five more hours of flight time it cannot be flown on a six-hour flight.

This is not all! She also handles crew scheduling when something goes wrong and in doing this must consider who is sick, on vacation, having a day off, or has used up flight hours. Then there is the problem of seniority bids, for she cannot schedule a pilot to fly a New York to Boston trip if he has bid and been checked out on a New York to Houston run.

"Of course I don't do all this alone," she confessed. "There are many others who help but the person who sits here is in charge and if anything goes wrong, they know who is to blame."

After we thanked Ms. Philips she directed us to our next interview with Edward Carlino, the meteorologist on duty, who was also expecting us.

METEOROLOGIST

The meteorologist's small office was adjacent to the flight operations office. Weather charts covered most of the walls and two teletype machines stood in one corner of the room. As we introduced ourselves one of them started to chatter.

"That's the weather facsimile machine," Mr. Carlino explained. "See, it prints out an exact reproduction of the latest weather map which has been prepared in Washington. The other one prints messages that come in from all over the system. Many of them give weather or other information I can use in my work."

He motioned for us to sit and told us that his job was to analyze weather data and prepare up-to-date weather reports for the flight dispatcher, the pilots, and others who need weather information ". . . like the ramp manager who wants to know if it's going to snow because it raises the dickens with his people. Actually, as you have probably already learned, one of my most important responsibilities is to work with the pilots and help them prepare their flight plans. What we are always looking for is a way to fly the most direct route but one which will have calm weather to ensure a smooth ride and, if possible, avoid headwinds because they require more fuel. It's a large order, and sitting in this little office it sometimes takes a bit of detective work to find out exactly how we should route a plane all the way from New York to Seattle or Mexico."

A college degree with a major in meteorology is necessary to qualify for this job, Mr. Carlino told us. "As a matter of fact," he added, "some airlines may also require previous experience with the United States Weather Bureau or one of the military weather services."

OTHER POSITIONS IN THE DEPARTMENT

"Since it's getting late and the general operations offices are closed, could you give us some idea of the overall organization one might expect to find in an airline operations department?" we asked Mr. Carlino.

"Let's see, I would say that you could pretty well divide the department into two main parts: aircraft sales and services and flight operations. The aircraft sales and services division sells surplus airplanes to other airlines and arranges to provide maintenance and other services for airlines which do not compete."

"This is a new development in air transportation, and it makes a lot of sense. Suppose a large airline flies to Kansas City, which is also served by a small regional carrier. It's uneconomic for both companies to duplicate all their services. Thus the larger company could sell tickets for the regional carrier, handle their passenger boarding and baggage, as well as service their airplanes. All the regional carrier would have to do is provide its own airplanes and flight crews."

"As for the flight department, you will usually find various specialists heading up divisions such as crew schedule, flight dispatch, operations analysis, flight instruction, flight administration, and perhaps more, depending on how much a company wants to break down the operations functions.

"By the way, I should mention that we employ radio operators who may be hired after receiving special training in a technical school and obtaining their radio operators' licenses. An operator is always on duty to take messages from the pilots and to contact them if necessary. Each airplane has its own code number and by typing that number into a keyboard connected to the radio transmitter, the radio operator can call that particular plane without bothering other aircraft. Many airlines also use the services of Aeronautical Radio, Incorporated, a nonprofit company which provides similar services to the airlines.

"One of the most important divisions is the flight training division. Which reminds me," and he sat up straight, tilting his chair back slightly, "you should make some notes about the flight instructor. Let me tell you about that position."

FLIGHT INSTRUCTOR

"Flight safety is of the greatest concern to everyone in the operations department," Mr. Carlino began. "That is why so much emphasis is placed on training flight crews. In the old days an airplane had to be used just to train crews and this was expensive. Once the computer was developed, however, it became possible to make what is called a 'flight simulator.' This is a mock-up of an airplane cockpit exactly like that on a real airplane, complete with seats, instrument panels, controls, and windows.

The pilot who is being trained sits in the pilot's seat and looks ahead through the window at a screen on which he or she sees a simulated runway. The simulator creates a precise, full-color, moving image of what pilots really see when landing or taking off and this simulation can be created for hundreds of airports all over the world. When the aircraft starts to 'move' it looks as though it were actually rolling down the runway. A control panel nearby enables the instructor to put the airplane through all sorts of maneuvers. Thus the pilot takes the plane up off the runway and just as the aircraft gets airborne, the instructor makes two of the engines fail. The pilot must make an immediate decision and take corrective action. The instructor can tell exactly what the student does and whether or not it is the right response. In this way all sorts of emergencies can be simulated and practiced without any danger whatsoever. Of course the pilot is also checked out regularly in an airplane but it is not necessary to risk an accident by putting it through dangerous maneuvers.

"Instructors teach flight crew members when they first join the company and continue to train and check them after they have started working. To qualify for these jobs one must have had at least two years of airline experience as well as some teaching experience.

"I think it's safe to say that the operations department is like most other departments in an airline," Mr. Carlino continued. "High school graduates can find beginning positions in clerical jobs, ramp work, and other areas, and for those who have had more education or special training, better jobs are frequently available. There are many interesting openings from time to time throughout the department for men and women who are willing to start near the bottom and work their way up. And that reminds me of one more division which will interest you although it isn't part of the operations department—still it's right here and we work closely with these people. That's the food service division," he glanced up at the clock, "and we can still visit the kitchen if you'd like. I always enjoy showing it off to visitors but daytime is the best time to go there—that's when the kitchen's a noisy, busy place!"

FOOD SERVICE DIVISION

We followed Mr. Carlino as he led the way to the opposite end of the building and through a short hallway into the largest kitchen we had ever seen. Long tables filled much of the space and several kitchen ranges were lined up across the far end. A baker dressed in white uniform and wearing a chef's hat was peering into an oven. Walk-in refrigerators and storage rooms lined one wall, while dishwashers, sinks, and counters lined the other. Several desks, filing cabinets, and storage cabinets were arranged in the area near us. The stainless steel equipment shone, the floor was spotless, and a delicious smell of fresh-baked buns filled the air.

"There aren't many working now," Mr. Carlino observed as we watched a dozen men and women who were placing china and silverware on small plastic trays. "They're getting breakfast trays ready for early morning flights," he explained. "Shortly before flight time they'll put the cooked food in either hot or refrigerated containers and when it is time to serve, the flight attendants will dish the food."

Down an aisle between the serving tables and near the far wall were the dishwashers. "They're cleaning up the china and silverware that came off flights which arrived this evening." Mr. Carlino said. "The main kitchen crew works during the daytime. The only food that might go out now would be cold beverages, coffee, and snacks. The last evening flight on which dinner is served leaves by seven-thirty and those meals must be ready no later than quarter of seven to get them loaded on the food service truck and taken over to the airplane. After that, there's little activity here."

The baker, who had just taken a pan of buns from the oven, came over to offer each of us a hot sample. "Passengers always love 'em," he said with evident pride, "and it's fun to cook and bake when you know people appreciate what you do."

"Good food is terribly important," Mr. Carlino agreed. Eating is one of the fun parts of flying for many passengers and they are quick to complain if there's anything wrong with the food. Incidentally, this a a good place for high school graduates to start because they will be trained on the job. All a young person needs is a health certificate, an interest in food preparation, and respect for good housekeeping procedures. A man or woman can advance eventually to pantry worker, steward chef, supervisor, chief chef, assistant buyer, or commissary chef. There's usually a lot of turnover in commissaries and those who stay and apply themselves can win advancement."

It was getting late, so we thanked the baker and asked Mr. Carlino to direct us back to the crew car. Laughing, he told us we'd never find it without a guide, and five minutes later we were saying good-bye and shaking hands with him as the driver came by to pick us up, for the trip back to the terminal.

The snow had stopped, the stars were shining, and we could hear a jet taking off across the airport. We wondered how the station manager and his assistant at Philadelphia were making out by now.

Powerplant mechanics service each aircraft regularly for the safest possible operation. Photo: Delta Air Lines.

CHAPTER 9

THE AIRLINE MECHANIC

During aviation's infancy the entire maintenance department of an airline might have consisted of one or two mechanics at either end of the run. It was their job to check the planes, see that they were functioning properly, and fix anything that was broken or not working properly. The work might have been done on the apron or in a hangar which probably was shared with owners of small planes. No one at that time could have dreamed of the huge maintenance depots that are operated by the airlines today, let alone the stringent maintenance regulations laid down by the Federal Aviation Administration as well as by the airlines themselves.

During those early days mechanics did not have any special training. They learned by doing and if they were good automobile mechanics, chances were that they could learn quickly what they needed to know about an airplane. Since then there has been great change. Airplane mechanics, who are also called professional aviation technicians, are highly trained individuals who are specially licensed by the Federal Aviation Administration to repair and maintain our nation's fleet of commercial airplanes as well as aircraft owned and operated by others.

THE MECHANIC'S LICENSE

It takes time, study, and hard work to earn your mechanic's license. Two ratings may be obtained by an airline mechanic: airframe (the body of an airplane) and power plant (the engine). Most people entering the aviation field have both ratings so that they can take advantage of many opportunities offered by the industry. There are three ways you can gain this all-important document:

1. *On-the-job training.* A few people become mechanics through this means and for these trainee jobs, employers prefer high school graduates who are in good physical condition and who have had experience in automobile repair work or other mechanical work.
2. *Training in the armed forces.* Those who were aircraft mechanics in one of the armed forces usually find that they have earned credit towards the work experience and other requirements for the license. Therefore they usually only need to attend a shorter program at one of the trade schools to learn procedures which pertain to civilian and commercial aircraft before taking the Federal Aviation Administration licensing test.
3. *Training in a school certified by the Federal Aviation Administration.* This is the route most men and women take who want to become airline mechanics. In an aviation technical school there is opportunity to work on real airplanes and complete practical projects under the guidance of qualified instructors in addition to receiving academic instruction. The minimum amount of time required to complete the course is 1,150 hours for an airframe rating; 1,150 hours for a power plant rating; and 1,900 hours for both ratings.

Before taking the Federal Aviation Administration examination, there must be proof of at least eighteen months' work experience for each license or thirty months' experience for both licenses, or graduation from an approved aviation mechanic's training school. The applicant also must be at least 18 years of age, and be able to read, write, and speak the English language.

One should be certain he or she has the interest as well as the aptitude to grasp the subject matter of the many courses which must be studied, before enrolling for training. Here is a typical course of study for becoming a licensed aviation technician as detailed by the Aviation Maintenance Foundation:

1. *General:* Basic Electricity; Aircraft Drawings; Weight and Balance; Fluid Lines and Fittings; Materials and Processes; Ground Operation and Servicing; Cleansing and Corrosion Control; Mathematics; Maintenance Forms and Records; Basic Physics; Maintenance Publications; Mechanic Privileges and Limitations.
2. *Airframe Structures:* Wood Structures; Aircraft Covering; Aircraft Finishes; Sheet Metal Structures; Welding; Assembly and Rigging; Airframe Inspection.
3. *Airframe Systems and Components:* Aircraft Landing Gear Systems; Hydraulic and Pneumatic Power Systems; Cabin Atmosphere Control Systems; Aircraft Instrument Systems; Communication and Navigation Systems; Aircraft Fuel Sys-Systems; Aircraft Electrical Systems; Position and Warning Systems; Ice and Rain Control Systems; Fire Protection Systems.
4. *Powerplant Theory and Maintenance:* Reciprocating Engines; Turbine Engines; Engine Inspection.
5. *Powerplant Systems and Components:* Engine Instrument Systems; Engine Fire Protection Systems; Engine Electrical Systems; Lubricating Systems; Ignition Systems; Fuel Metering Systems; Engine Fuel Systems; Induction Systems; Engine Cooling Systems; Engine Exhaust Systems, Propellers.

For a list of approved Aviation Maintenance Technical Training Schools or information regarding training facilities, tuition, required books and supplies, and available financing, write: Careers, Aviation Maintenance Foundation, P.O. Box 2826, Redmond, Washington 98073.

NATURE OF THE MECHANIC'S WORK

Some mechanics specialize in repairs. It might happen that during the preflight check of an airplane the pilot finds the gas gauge does not work. Because passengers are coming on board, the airplane's departure must not be delayed, so the mechanics must think and work quickly. The electrical connections must be checked with electrical test equipment to make sure no wires are shorted or cut. If these tests do not reveal the cause of the failure they may replace the gauge, working as fast as safety permits so that the plane will be ready to operate as soon as possible. After an airplane has completed its trip a mechanic reviews the pilot's report of any difficulty so that the faulty equipment can be repaired.

Scheduled maintenance is handled by other mechanics. All planes are inspected and different types of maintenance are performed according to a schedule based on the number of hours the aircraft has flown, calendar days, or a combination of these factors. These mechanics may examine the engines through specially designed openings as they work standing on ladders or scaffolds, or it may be necessary to remove the entire engine from the plane by using hoists or fork lifts. Other mechanics may take the engine apart, then measure the various parts for wear by using delicate instruments, check for invisible cracks with x-ray and magnetic inspection equipment, and replace worn parts. They may also repair sheet metal surfaces, measure the tension of all control cables, and check for distortion, rust, and cracks in parts of the fuselage and wings. Once repairs are made, the mechanics test the equipment to make sure that the repairs were made properly.

At certain points along an airline system, line maintenance is performed, usually at the larger stations where there is adequate hangar space. This maintenance consists of periodic checks and servicing of various parts of the airplane and its power plant. For major maintenance and overhaul the airplanes are sent to what is usually a very large facility, a "maintenance base," which may consist of several huge buildings, each capable of holding several aircraft and containing sophisticated machine shops and every conceivable kind of equipment required for the extensive repair and refurbishing work undertaken. In each of these facilities hundreds of mechanics and others are employed.

As noted previously mechanics are among the most essential of all airline employees. The safety of every flight depends upon how well all of the mechanics performed their jobs. A loose nut, a missing bolt, an imperfect fit could spell disaster in the air.

ADDITIONAL TRAINING EARNS ADVANCEMENT

The first step in advancement can be achieved after you have your Federal Aviation Administration licenses and have had three years of experience. At that point you may receive your "Inspection Authorization" which makes you a "mechanic's mechanic"—one authorized to inspect and approve the work of other mechanics. This brings a higher rate of pay and more recognition.

The course of advancement is usually from mechanic to head mechanic or crew chief, to inspector, to head inspector, to shop supervisor. A few supervisors may rise to executive positions.

Advanced training is also available in the form of specialized factory training. Many manufacturers offer advanced training in a facility right at the factory. With this additional education you may specialize in fields that include jet turbines, propellers, interior design and upholstery, aircraft painting, maintenance of helicopters, nondestructive testing, and many others.

There is keen competition for these jobs. The fact that mechanics are so well paid has made it an attractive profession. Therefore it is difficult at times to find a job because there are more qualified applicants than job openings and from time to time when airline business slacks off and schedules are cut back, mechanics are laid off and placed on furlough. Do not let this discourage you, however. When the time comes for you to get your mechanic's training, find out about employment prospects by writing the personnel departments of two or three airlines.

JOBS IN GENERAL AVIATION

If airline job prospects are slim, try general aviation; private companies which operate airports, provide certain flight services, and run repair shops; corporations which have their own fleets of aircraft; the forestry service, state fish and game departments; municipalities; and the federal government, which employs civilian mechanics in the military as well as at the Federal Aviation Administration headquarters in Oklahoma City.

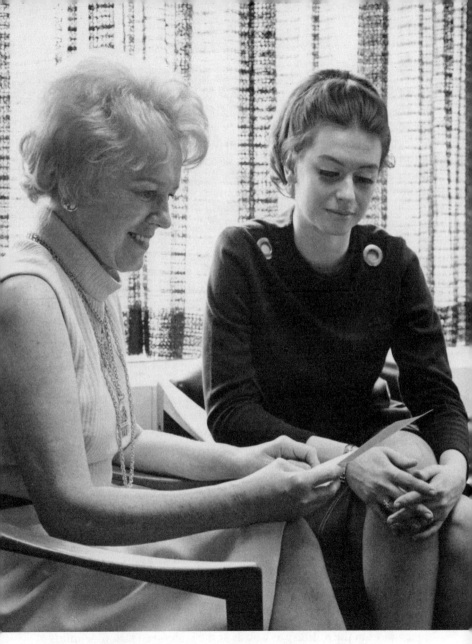

The personnel department interviews prospective employees and administers corporate programs for wages, benefits, and training. Photo: Secretaries, Inc.

CHAPTER 10

THE PERSONNEL DEPARTMENT

Since people are the most important part of any airline, it has been found that the services of the personnel department are as essential to the successful operation of a company as those of an efficient reservations department.

PERSONNEL AND LABOR RELATIONS WORKERS

Personnel workers and labor relations workers are the link between employees and management at all levels. They help keep employees satisfied with their jobs, pay, and working conditions, and at the same time enable management to make the most effective use of the employees' skills. In carrying out their duties, the personnel workers interview, select, and recommend applicants for job openings, handle wage and salary administration, employee benefits, and training and career development. The labor relations workers, on the other hand, specialize in carrying out union-management relations which means they help airline officials prepare for collective bargaining sessions, usually represent the management in negotiating contracts with the unions, and handle a multitude of labor relations matters which come up daily.

You will find a sizable personnel department in a large airline. It may include on its staff the following categories of specialists: recruiters, interviewers, counselors, job analysts, wage and salary analysts, education and training specialists, labor relations specialists, clerks, stenographers, and typists.

Because personnel work deals with people, their welfare, and their problems, if you plan to enter this field you should like people, enjoy helping them and working with them, and have a congenial and persuasive personality. You also need to be able to empathize, which means to understand the feelings and ideas of the other person. You should have a great reservoir of patience too, because many of the people with whom you deal will be unsure of themselves, suspicious of you, and have difficulty reaching a decision, while a few will be stubborn or deceitful. At the same time you must be able to keep confidences and avoid becoming emotionally involved in others' problems. As a representative of management, you always keep the company's position and policies foremost in mind when you deal with situations in which you are trying to be fair in your treatment of the employee.

To make the personnel functions more meaningful, let's consider the principal specialists you will find in a large airline. Bear in mind that the smaller the airline, the smaller the department and the more responsibilities fewer staff members must assume.

PERSONNEL RECRUITER OR EMPLOYMENT INTERVIEWER

When airlines experience periods of business expansion they soon need additional flight attendants, mechanics, and any number of other specialists. At such times they may send personnel recruiters out to schools and colleges to interview prospective applicants. You might first meet one of these interviewers if you were in a junior college and an airline was looking for flight attendants, or if you were studying at an aviation maintenance training school and an interviewer was scheduled to come talk with students who were about to graduate. On the other hand you might pick up your local newspaper and see an advertisement announcing that interviews will be given to applicants seeking positions as flight attendants and mechanics on a certain day at a hotel, civic center, or other building in the business section of your city.

When you go for your interview (whether away from or at the airline employment office) you will first be asked to fill out an application form which requests details about your background, education, special skills, interests, and work experience. The interviewer will then talk with you and perhaps give you a test or two which he or she will interpret and grade. It will then be up to the interviewer to decide whether or not you will be recommended for consideration by the head of the department that is seeking additional employees.

You will observe that the interviewer is familiar with the work of the department as well as the company's personnel policies, wage scales, employee benefits, and prospects for promotion. What you might not be aware of is the mental assessment that will be made of you as he or she talks with you, or the fact that the interviewer must be exceedingly careful to comply with the various laws governing employment and the provisions of the Equal Opportunities laws. In fact some companies have men and women on their personnel staff who are specialists in interpreting these laws.

JOB ANALYST: WAGE AND SALARY ADMINISTRATOR

Whenever the head of a department wishes to create a new job or change an existing one, the personnel department is notified, and a job analyst is assigned to study the request. The analyst sits down with the department head or representative and obtains detailed information about the job such as the qualifications specified, the duties of the job, the training and skills which may be required, and any unusual working conditions. The job analyst then studies this data and prepares a job description.

The wage and salary administrator, another specialist, then studies the job description, and by applying salary standards and pay scales which have been set up, decides which pay scale fits the newly created position. In addition he or she may also study the overall salary scales and schedules of pay increases to make certain that the rates are fair and obey government laws and regulations. Every employee covered by a union contract must be paid in accordance with the provisions of the latest agreement. Wage and salary administrators also study national cost-of-living trends and recommend general wage adjustments to management when it seems advisable. Another duty is to conduct surveys to see how the company's pay scales compare with those of other airlines. Most companies readily exchange this information on a confidential basis.

EMPLOYEE BENEFITS SECTION

Responsibilities in this section gradually increase as an airline extends more and more benefits to its employees. The most important include health insurance, life insurance, disability insurance, and pension plans. Although these group insurance programs may be administered by either the finance or personnel department, the personnel department is responsible for seeing that every employee is told about the programs and given opportunity to enroll if membership is optional. In the case of the airlines, one of the most important benefits is the reduced transportation fares which every employee is entitled to receive after being on the payroll for a certain period of time. The number of trips one may take increases with seniority, hence detailed records must be kept for every employee! Retired personnel also have free transportation privileges, and this entails issuing annual passes and processing special requests for retirees.

The benefits section usually coordinates a number of employee services including newsletters, employee cafeterias and snack bars, recreation programs, and credit unions. It is also responsible for counseling employees on work-related problems as well as giving pre-retirement counseling to those employees expecting to retire soon.

MEDICAL SECTION

Most airlines have a medical section because of the requirement to give flight personnel periodical examinations. Various members of management may also be eligible for free physical examinations which are given by company physicians or in some cases at private health clinics. A company doctor and nursing staff may be on duty at a large facility to give examinations and treat emergencies. However, there is only a limited need for physicians and registered nurses since most airline offices are located close to hospitals or other medical offices.

LABOR RELATIONS SECTION

The labor relations section is one of the most interesting, challenging, and often frustrating areas of personnel work. In an airline, a labor relations section must deal with several unions and this means that much of the time the staff is preparing for the next lengthy and usually exhausting session of bargaining. This is when representatives of the company and the union sit opposite each other for "collective bargaining" and discuss each of the union's requests, sometimes called "demands." The most important topics usually concern the union's requests for increased pay, shorter working hours, additional holidays, improved employee benefits, and better working conditions. During the course of the bargaining the union representatives generally ask for more than they expect to win, while company representatives offer less than they are prepared to give. This enables each party to bargain and give a little now and then as they try to reach an agreement. If they fail, the union may call a strike once the old contract has expired. A strike of pilots will close down an airline and require massive layoffs of employees. At times like this the labor relations section works around-the-clock doing everything it can to get the bargaining talks started again so that a decision can be reached and striking employees returned to work. These can be frantic days and nights when tempers become short and frustrations grow. Disputes are always settled sooner or later, however, and the labor relations staff resumes its normal activities, some of which are described below.

Labor relations is becoming an increasingly important part of personnel administration. This is especially true in airlines because of the number of unions which represent employees. Personnel departments therefore need specialists skilled in handling negotiations and grievances, and in interpreting the terms of union contracts. Labor relations specialists must have extensive knowledge of economics, labor law, collective bargaining trends, and company personnel policies. When a labor agreement is about to expire and negotiations for a new contract open between the company and the union, the director of the labor relations section will usually represent the company. The director is assisted by a staff of experts who are constantly on hand during the negotiating sessions and provide any additional information needed.

Once the contract has been approved, members of the labor relations section must make certain that all of the provisions are made known to each department which has union members on its payroll. Inevitably there will be misunderstandings, disputes, and disagreements about the meaning or application of the contract provisions. These must be worked out between the labor relations staff and the union.

At other times there may be problems caused by a general layoff and this can occasion a labor dispute because seniority rights of union members become an issue. Occasionally a union shop steward may request a hearing about a grievance involving a union member, and other controversies involving union-management relations are bound to occur from time to time. Administering labor relations is a job that calls for a thorough knowledge of current developments in labor law, the ability to interpret a contract, and a fine sense of fairness, patience, and understanding.

Unions also employ labor relations specialists. An elected union official may handle labor relations problems with the company, but the national and international union headquarters employ research and labor relations specialists just as the airlines do.

It should be noted here that many of the newer "cut-rate" airlines which have sprung up since deregulation are nonunion. This enables them to pay whatever wages they wish without having to negotiate contracts with unions representing several categories of employees. The influence and membership of many unions generally have been decreasing during the last several years. This has been true in the airline industry too, except in the case of the major long-established carriers where the unions are firmly entrenched.

The fact that an airline is non-union should not keep you from considering it when you seek a job. The wage and salary rates of such companies may be lower than those paid by unionized carriers, but that does not necessarily make these companies less attractive employers otherwise. Job opportunities and careers will be found within these enterprises too, and you may find they meet your needs.

PREPARING FOR A CAREER IN PERSONNEL WORK

Most employers look for college graduates to fill beginning positions in personnel and labor relations. Others prefer graduates who have majored in personnel administration or industrial and labor relations, and some seek a general business background. A well-rounded liberal arts education satisfies some employers but certainly a college degree in personnel administration, political science, or public administration is an asset in looking for a job.

Many colleges and universities offer programs leading to a degree in the field of personnel and labor relations but the number of programs which concentrate on labor relations is relatively small. If you are interested in personnel work you might consider courses in personnel management, psychology, public administration, economics, statistics, and sociology. If labor relations is your choice, you should consider labor law, collective bargaining, labor economics, labor history, and industrial psychology courses for your preparation. A top position in labor relations may call for graduate study in industrial or labor relations and a law degree is usually required for those who negotiate contracts.

A college education is not the only way to prepare to enter personnel work, however. It is possible to start at the clerical level and work one's way up to a professional position as experience is gained and college courses are taken at night.

Once employed on your first job you may be given on-the-job training to acquaint you with the company and its personnel policies. You will also be shown how to classify jobs, interview applicants, or administer employee benefits. You will then be assigned to an area in the employee relations department. It may be possible to change your specialty if that seems desirable or perhaps even move

Uniforms are required for many airline employment positions; sometimes the uniforms are unusual, like these special tropical uniforms for United Airlines' continental U.S.1-to-Hawaii flights. Photo. United Airlines.

over to labor relations work. Those who enter labor relations work directly following formal education programs are usually graduates of Master's degree programs in industrial relations or possible attorneys who have recently earned their law degrees. In either case new employees probably will start out as trainees, working under the guidance and supervision of an experienced member of the labor relations section.

At one time, many employers looked upon the personnel department as a necessary evil but this is no longer true. Today progressive managements realize the benefits that can be gained from good labor/management relations and therefore are willing to support sound employee relations programs carried out by capable staffs.

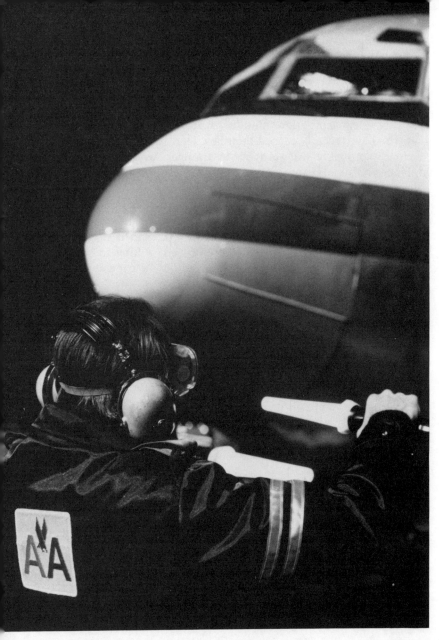

Many airline workers—like this ground crew member, for example—do not have to travel as part of their work. Photo: United Airlines.

CHAPTER 11

JOB OPPORTUNITIES AT AIRPORTS

When airlines were first carrying passengers, "Let's go out to the airport," was a popular suggestion made in thousands of homes on Sunday afternoons. All across the country people would drive to the nearest field, park their cars, and watch the planes take off and land. Then, as aviation grew, many larger airports built visitors' observation decks and charged ten cents admission. Whole families would go and make their visit a day's outing.

Few people today go to the airport for a Sunday afternoon diversion. Most of the larger airports are so crowded it is no pleasure to buck the traffic. More to the point, however, is the fact that so many people have either flown, met friends at airports, or seen them off, that it is no longer much of a novelty.

Although airports are as necessary to an airline as the airplanes it owns and flies, airlines do not own major airports. Most airports belong to and are operated by the municipal governments of the cities they serve, by airport authorities, counties, or some other governmental agency.

A number of the smaller airports are owned and operated by individuals or companies. Regardless of who may own the smaller airports, here we find an entirely different world—the world of the fixed base operator serving general aviation—small aircraft owned by individuals and companies.

Because of the opportunities small airports can offer in starting a career in aviation or airport management, we shall briefly explain the role of the fixed base operator, often referred to in the trade as the FBO.

FBO: THE FIXED BASE OPERATOR

Just as the major airport is dependent on the large airlines for its business, so does the smaller airport with its fixed base operator (FBO) depend on general aviation which it is designed to serve. There are approximately 200,000 general aviation aircraft, all of which need fuel, parts, accessories, regular maintenance, overhauls, and storage. Many owners of these small airplanes also require pilots to fly them if they are not licensed pilots themselves, and a number of owners pilot their own planes or want to learn how to fly.

An FBO may employ one or one hundred workers. The two-person business may be conducted from a small hangar or shop with an office and a pilot's lounge, whereas an employer of a hundred people would have an impressive establishment consisting of shops, hangars, offices, classrooms, and showrooms where new aircraft could be purchased. The FBO may employ flight instructors, aviation mechanics, salespersons, and office personnel. The owner might also operate a small aviation mechanics training school, supervise the work of mechanics, and arrange for ground transportation and overnight accommodations for general aviation pilots and their passengers.

The size of an airport facility depends on the FBO's business ability, experience, amount of capital invested in the business, and willingness to work hard. Many operators start out working alone, then gradually build up a staff as business grows. Eventually some develop sizable operations which offer everything the owner of an airplane might need: aircraft sales, pilot instruction, aircraft fuel and parts, airframe and power plant maintenance and overhaul, and instrument repairs. In addition, FBOs may have one or more airplanes of their own which enable them to offer air taxi service and charter flights.

Many FBOs employ ramp service persons or "line persons" whose job responsibilities are to greet arriving airplanes, guide them to parking spots, help the pilots tie down or park the aircraft, fill the tanks with gas, check the oil, vacuum the cabin interior, wash the windshield and windows, and report to the owner any damage or problems that were observed. If you are in your teens this is a good way to enter aviation and start your career by working part-time under an FBO after school, on weekends, and during summers. Perhaps you could use your salary to finance flight training or study for your mechanic's rating. A line person's job can lead to many aviation careers associated with airport management or to positions as aviation mechanic, pilot, or even air traffic controller.

Moving from the small fields with their FBOs to the larger airports served by major airlines, we will consider some of the principal careers in airport operation and management which may interest you.

THE MAJOR AIRPORT IS MANY THINGS

In the transportation world today, there is nothing quite as exciting as an airport! Imagine a major field like Chicago's O'Hare, Los Angeles' International, New York's Kennedy, or Dallas/Ft. Worth's huge new facility where thousands of people work and where just as many come and go each day as flight after flight takes off and lands with a regularity and precision that seems like the most normal thing in the world. Meanwhile a constant stream of buses, automobiles, trucks, and vans rush across the vast network of roads while all kinds of tractors, jeeps, baggage trains, gasoline trucks, and other vehicles scurry between terminals and hangars as they service the fleets of aircraft and carry airline employees from one place to another. Perhaps the most remarkable thing about these airports is the way all the different functions mesh and work together to help produce what we commonly think of as air transportation. Few people are aware of how complicated an airport really is or of the many organizations which combine efforts to make it function smoothly.

We are now familiar with the airlines and how their employees function at the airport as they take care of the passengers, handle the baggage and freight, and service the aircraft. The men and women in the air traffic control tower are also very much a part of the airport, although they work apart from the terminal and hangar areas. The stores, restaurants, coffee shops, barber shops, car rental agencies, and other concessions which cater to travelers in the terminals provide essential airport services too. Finally, there are the terminal buildings, hangars, roads, landing strips, and ramps which are maintained by the airport management. Actually the airlines, the restaurants, and other concessions rent their space from the airport which is the landlord and owner of all the facilities. The individual responsible for the overall operation of an airport is the director, a job which carries a tremendous responsibility, as we shall see.

THE AIRPORT DIRECTOR

A director of an airport which serves major airlines should have a college degree in one of the following areas: airport management, business administration, public administration, aeronautical or civil engineering. Airport managers themselves have rated as "very important" the following education subject areas: public relations, air transportation, business management and personnel administration. If your goal is to head up a large airport some day, it is not too soon to start thinking now about how to prepare yourself for that big job!

To reach the top position in a major airport one must have had prior experience as a director or assistant director at an airport. Directors of small airports may qualify in some cases (even though they have only a high school diploma) if they hold a pilot's license and have had three to five years' experience in several types of jobs associated with airport services such as superintendent of maintenance, assistant to the airport director, or fixed base operator. An airport director must be familiar with state and federal air regulations—especially those pertaining to airports—zoning laws, legal contracts, public relations, use of airport equipment, the proper handling of aircraft, and airline operations. He or she must have administrative and leadership qualities, ability to get along with others, tact, initiative, and good judgment.

An airport director has been described as "a mixture of aviation expert, real estate operator, construction engineer, electronics wizard, management genius, and politician." Perhaps this is because the director is expected to be knowledgeable about almost everything pertaining to an airport. These are the principal responsibilities:

- administering the overall management of the airport
- training and supervising the employees who report to the director
- setting up the airport budget
- keeping records and making required reports
- planning and supervising maintenance programs
- negotiating leases with tenants such as airlines, concessionaries, and aircraft repair stations
- making and enforcing airport rules and regulations
- promoting the use of the airport
- surveying the future needs of the airport

Just as airports vary greatly in size, so do the staffs of their directors. The individual in charge of a very small airport may have only one assistant whereas at a large facility, there might be a staff consisting of an assistant director, an engineer, controller, personnel officer, public relations officer, a maintenance superintendent, and a large number of support employees.

Many universities offer degrees in airport administration, public administration, business administration, and aeronautical or civil engineering. Some also offer flight training which, in conjunction with airport administration courses, provides an extensive knowledge of aviation and the role of the airport.

There are only approximately one thousand airports employing full-time directors. Therefore, it is only sensible to consider jobs which are attainable on the director's staff and which can also offer highly rewarding careers. You may be interested in writing to the American Association of Airport Executives, 4224 King Street, Alexandria, VA 22302, for a copy of their publication, *Airport Management—A Profession.*

AIRPORT JOBS

The usual duties expected of a controller, personnel manager, public relations director, treasurer, secretary, typist, clerk, receptionist, and switchboard operator are performed by office personnel on the airport director's staff. An assistant director carries out many of the administrative duties and may be in charge of all the maintenance and other employees, as well as responsible for airport tenant relations. Depending on the size of the airport, educational qualifications for the assistant director's job range from a high school diploma to an engineering degree. Larger airports would look for three to seven years of prior engineering experience in a job applicant.

A crew of service specialists works under the direction of the airport manager, the assistant, or the engineer. The crew may do one or more of the following: operate snow removal equipment; cut grass and maintain shrubbery; fill holes, level low places and bumps on runways and taxiways; service runway lights and replace defective fuses and lamps; maintain electrical service; paint buildings; do general carpentry work; and clean the building interiors and exteriors. At a large airport there would probably be an airport electrician and assistants, a carpenter and assistants, and members of other trades and crafts, whereas at a small airport one or two employees might perform all of these jobs, or the manager might contract with an outside maintenance service to do this work.

Among the safety and security employees are trained firefighters and rescue workers who are always on duty ready with their fire-fighting and crash rescue equipment. Some of these employees may also be required to inspect the airport for fire hazards and report violations of airport fire regulations. Previous experience as a fire-fighter would be desirable to qualify for this work. Security guards may or may not need prior experience to be considered for openings.

Information about job opportunities at an airport can best be gotten from the "Help Wanted" advertisements in your newspaper and by visiting the airport. At the director's office ask how you may apply for employment. If it is a small airport the director or the secretary will probably talk with you, but in the case of a large facility you can expect to be referred to the personnel department.

When you seek employment at an airport remember that the concessions mentioned at the bottom of page 121 also offer job opportunities and a possible way of getting your start at an airport.

THE OUTLOOK FOR THE FUTURE

Forecasts for the future in air transportation predict large increases in the number of passengers and air-freight tonnage, as well as the use of general aviation aircraft. Existing airports will have to be enlarged and new ones built. As new airfields open, there will be need for additional fixed base operators with resulting employment opportunities for a wide range of skilled men and women. It is also expected that "satellite" airports will be constructed near major airports. All this spells more openings for those interested in pursuing a career in some phase of airport management, or in any of the other positions mentioned above.

The computer revolution has made the job of these air traffic controllers much easier than it used to be. Photo: Delta Air Lines.

CHAPTER 12

AIR TRAFFIC CONTROL

On a summer day in 1956 two aircraft left the Los Angeles International Airport three minutes apart. This was a normal procedure and both planes soon turned east to fly along the established air routes over southern California and into Arizona. Suddenly they flew beyond radio contact with the ground stations and into airspace that was not controlled. Four miles above the Grand Canyon, they collided and crashed, killing all 128 passengers and crew.

REGIONAL CONTROL CENTERS

Immediately following this tragic accident, the government started work on a vastly improved air traffic control system which depended on a network of radar antennas, some 133 of them altogether. Today an airplane is constantly in view of two or more radarscopes and its location is accurately plotted on the scopes of one of the twenty regional air route traffic control centers. In addition, an elaborate computer system tracks all of the aircraft and warns of any possible midair collisions. To see how this system works let us follow the progress of Captain Tracy Bigelow's flight, which was scheduled to take off from Kennedy International Airport at four o'clock for Los Angeles.

By three o'clock Captain Bigelow had completed his flight plan and his airline filed it with the New York Air Route Traffic Control Center at Ronkonkoma, Long Island. There the plan was programmed into a computer, which checked to see if it conflicted with any other proposed traffic leaving Kennedy at four o'clock. It then automatically transmitted information about the plane to the departure controllers at TRACON, the terminal radar approach control facility, and to the Kennedy tower.

At exactly four o'clock the plane pulled away from the loading gate. As it taxied slowly from the terminal building, Captain Bigelow radioed the tower for taxiing instructions and clearance for takeoff. The tower gave him his clearance based on the information previously relayed to it by the regional control center. After the plane was airborne, the tower told Captain Bigelow that he was being handed over to the TRACON departure controller who had already been following the flight.

TRACON is headquartered in a new complex at Garden City, Long Island. The most important part of the TRACON operation is the large darkened room with its rows of radar screens where all the traffic coming into and leaving the New York metropolitan airports can be seen as small "blips." A three or four person team works at a radar screen. Next to each blip is a "data block" which moves with the blip and tells the name of the airline, the flight number, the assigned altitude, and the current altitude. All this information is automatically fed into the screen by radio waves which are sent out by each airplane and received by the large radar antennas which continuously sweep the sky.

When Captain Bigelow's plane had flown west about forty miles he was told that he was cleared to continue his climb to "three-five-zero" (35,000 feet). From here on, as the flight crossed the country, it would move from one radarscope sector to another. Each air traffic control center is responsible for a region which may have as many as thirty or forty sectors, with a team of controllers monitoring each sector. As a plane nears the boundary between two sectors the computer flashes an "H" in the data block to tell the next sector that the flight is approaching. Those working the console in the next sector check to make certain there are no problems or possible conflicts and then accept control by flashing an "O" in the data block of the flight before it leaves the previous sector.

Captain Bigelow's flight passed from sector to sector as it proceeded across the country. At any time if the plane were to start converging with the route of another plane, the computer would issue a "conflict alert" in the data blocks of each plane. The controller would then order one of the pilots to change course.

When Captain Bigelow's plane entered the Los Angeles Control Center, he was given instructions on which way to descend and at what speed. Some fifty miles from Los Angeles the regional center gave control over to the Los Angeles Terminal Control Center, which thereafter instructed the captain on his descent right to his touchdown. The airplane taxied toward the terminal while the blip and data block disappeared from the screen, marking just one more flight guided safely to its destination over one of the most remarkable and sophisticated—but human-guided—systems the world has ever seen!

THE FEDERAL AVIATION ADMINISTRATION

The greatest number of aviation jobs found within the federal government, outside the Department of Defense, is offered by the Federal Aviation Administration (FAA) of the Department of Transportation. The FAA, with approximately 46,000 employees, is charged with the administration and enforcement of all federal air regulations to ensure the safety of air transportation. The FAA also promotes, guides, and assists the development of a national system of civil airports. It provides pilots with flight information and air traffic control services from flight planning to landing.

All of the FAA aviation jobs come under the Federal Civil Service, and wage scales are determine by Congress. A normal workweek consists of forty hours, with additional payment (called premium pay) made for shift work involving duty between 6:00 p.m. and 6:00 a.m., and for work on Sunday and holidays. Merit promotions are awarded under provisions of a Civil Service approved merit promotion plan. Employees also participate in a liberal retirement plan, while health insurance, low-cost group life insurance, compensation and medical care for injury on the job and other benefits are offered.

Of all the job openings in the federal government probably those of air traffic control specialists are considered the most exciting and glamorous. Actually there are three types of specialists, as described below, but the educational and experience requirements for all are similar.

AIR TRAFFIC CONTROL SPECIALISTS

Although you cannot be over 30 years of age to start on the job, this is not a position you can move into right after graduating from college. Hence you should plan your education and early work experience to make certain that you acquire the necessary background to qualify for the job.

The Federal Aviation Administration says than an applicant must have a minimum of two years' *general* experience and, for the higher grades and more demanding positions, from one to three years *specialized* experience. This is how the Federal Aviation Administration defines the required background:

"General Experience: Progressively responsible experience in administrative, technical, or other work which demonstrated potential for learning and performing air traffic control work."

"Specialized Experience: Experience in a military or civilian air traffic facility which demonstrated possession of the knowledge, skills, and abilities required to perform the level of work of the specialization for which application is made."

It is possible to substitute certain education and flight training for experience. Therefore it would be well to request the latest regulations of the Federal Aviation Administration with regard to the qualifications for this job before planning your career future. The physical requirements are not overly stringent. "Applicants must be able to pass a physical examination (including normal color vision). Air traffic control specialists are required to requalify in a physical examination given annually."

Applicants must also pass a comprehensive written test and have a complete personal interview. Alertness, decisiveness, diction, poise, and conciseness of speech are evaluated during the course of the interview. Both men and women are employed, but few occupations make more rigid physical and mental demands on employees than that of air traffic controller. Because studies show that the unique skills necessary for success as a controller diminish with age, the maximum age of 30 was established without exception for entry into a Federal Aviation Administration tower or center controller position.

The nature of the work, the working conditions, and job location of the three specialist positions are as follows:

Air Traffic Control Specialist at FAA Airport Traffic Control Tower. The air traffic control specialists direct air traffic so that it will flow smoothly and efficiently. Controllers give pilots their taxiing and takeoff instruction, air traffic clearances, and advice about weather conditions based on information received from various sources. They transfer control of an airplane which is operated on instruments to the Air Route Traffic Control Center when the aircraft leaves their airspace, and they also receive data from the center regarding aircraft flying into their airspace. In addition these controllers also operate airport and runway lighting systems and prepare reports on air traffic and communications. They must be able to recall quickly registration numbers of airplanes under their control, the aircraft types and speeds, positions in the air, and also the location of navigational aids in their area.

The controllers normally work a forty-hour week in FAA control towers at airports using radio, radar, electronic computers, telephones, traffic control lights, and other devices for communication. Shift work is necessary and each controller is responsible at separate times for giving taxiing instructions to aircraft on the ground, takeoff instructions and air traffic clearances, and for directing landings of incoming planes. At busy locations these duties are rotated among the staff about every two hours. A controller must work quickly, and mental demands will increase as the traffic mounts, especially when poor flying conditions occur and traffic stacks up. Brief rest periods provide some relief but are not always possible. Radar controllers usually work in semi-darkness.

The FAA employs over 12,500 controllers at more than 400 airports. A few towers are located outside the continental United States in Alaska, Hawaii, Puerto Rico, the Virgin Islands, and American

Samoa. In 1983 the FAA began a ten year, $12 billion dollar program to upgrade air-traffic control equipment.

Promotion from trainee to a higher grade professional controller depends on the employee's performance and satisfactory progression in her or his training program. Trainees who do not successfully complete their training courses are separated or reassigned from their controller positions. During the first year a trainee is on probation and then may advance from positions backing up professional controllers to primary positions of responsibility. It takes a controller from three to six years of experience to reach the full performance level. Some professional controllers are selected for research activities with FAA's National Aviation Facilities Experimental Center in Atlantic City, New Jersey. Others are selected to serve as instructors at the FAA Academy in Oklahoma City, Oklahoma. Trainees receive from fifteen to nineteen weeks instruction at the FAA Academy and are then assigned to a tower for on-the-job training under close supervision until successful completion of the training period. From time to time the FAA conducts training to upgrade controllers, thus air traffic control training continues long after the controller has reached the full performance level.

Air Traffic Control Specialist at FAA Air Route Traffic Control Centers. The specialists give the pilots instruction, air traffic clearances, and advice regarding flight conditions along the flight path, while the pilot is flying the federal airways or approaching airports which do not have towers. The controllers use flight plans and keep track of the progress of all instrument flights within that center's airspace. They transfer control of aircraft on instrument flights to the controller in the next center when the plane enters that center's airspace and also monitor the arrival time of each airplane over various navigation fixes and maintain records of the flights under their control.

Using electronic computers, radio, radar, telephones, and other electronic communication devices, air route controllers work at FAA air route traffic control centers. They work in semidarkness and unlike the tower controllers never see the aircraft they control except as blips or "targets" on their radarscopes. Work is demanding in most areas. Registration numbers of all airplanes under control as well as types, speeds, and altitudes are automatically displayed on the radarscope, but each aircraft must be closely monitored to avoid other aircraft. Controllers are employed at some twenty-one air route traffic control centers located throughout the country, and in Guam, Panama, and Puerto Rico. For information on training see the first section describing the specialists who work at the FAA Airport Traffic Control Tower.

Air Traffic Control Specialist at FAA Flight Service Stations. These specialists render pre-flight, in-flight, and emergency assistance to pilots on request. They give information about actual weather conditions and forecasts for airports and flight paths, relay air traffic control instructions between controllers and pilots, assist pilots in emergency situations, and initiate searches for missing or overdue aircraft.

These specialist use telephones, radio, teletypewriters, direction finding and radar equipment. They work shifts in offices close to communications equipment with forty hours their normal workweek. The FAA flight service stations are found at nearly 300 airport locations throughout the United States, the Virgin Islands, and Puerto Rico,

Trainees are paid while they are learning their jobs, starting as a trainee in the flight service station and then advancing to assistant chief, deputy chief, or chief of the facility. A few positions at higher levels are available in FAA regional offices with administrative responsibilities over flight service stations in the area's jurisdiction.

It is not expected that the number of these specialists will increase as much as the jobs in other areas of air traffic control. With greater use of long distance telephones and other communications devices, flight service stations will serve larger areas. Nevertheless, these jobs will be more challenging as automation is more extensively introduced and they will become stepping-stones to air traffic controller careers in FAA airport traffic control towers and control centers.

ELECTRONIC TECHNICIAN

Electronic technicians install and maintain the complicated electronic equipment required for aerial navigation, communications between the aircraft and ground services, and control of aircraft movements. This involves working with radar, radio, computers, wire communication systems, and other electronic devices at airports and all along the network of federal airways. Technicians inspect equipment, read meters, replace deteriorating parts, adjust mechanisms not working properly, trouble-shoot, and repair and replace malfunctioning equipment. These technicians may also specialize in the design, development, and evaluation of new types of electronic equipment for the federal airways.

Most of the technicians are based at, and work out of, an Airway Facilities Sector Field Office with other technicians whose work is directed by a supervisor. The office may be located at an airport but the equipment for which the office is responsible may lie within a thirty or forty mile radius and be located in control towers, air route traffic control centers, flight service stations, or out in open fields or even on remote mountain tops. This means that some work must be done outdoors in all kinds of weather. Although forty hours is a normal workweek, shift work and weekend work are required. Thousands of electronic technicians are employed and there is opportunity to progress to supervisory positions and ultimately to managerial jobs at FAA headquarters.

Minimum entry age for this job is 18. Training and experience in electronics are required with a knowledge of basic electronic theory and related mathematics, transmitters and receivers, use of test equipment, techniques of trouble-shooting and circuitry analysis, use of tools, and installation practices.

Minimum experience of three years is required, but as with the specialists in controller jobs, some evaluation of education and specialized experience may be made. Applicants must also be able to pass a physical examination and be free from color blindness.

Technical and vocational schools offer courses in electronics, and upon assignment to an FAA sector office a new employee undergoes a short period of on-the-job training in which he or she is familiarized with FAA equipment and procedures. Technicians may receive three to four months instruction in any one year on new developments in the field of electronics at the FAA Academy in Oklahoma City.

Airspace system inspection technicians must meet the same employment requirements as electronic technicians, but they are required to fly in government aircraft as a member of a crew with airspace system inspection pilots during in-flight inspection of navigational aids.

OTHER JOBS WITH THE FAA

Aviation safety inspectors develop, administer, and enforce regulations and standards concerning civil aviation safety including the airworthiness of aircraft and aircraft systems, the competence of pilots, mechanics, and others and the safety aspects of aviation facilities, equipment, and procedures. For these positions you need knowledge and skill in the operation, maintenance, or manufacture of aircraft and aircraft systems. Again a minimum of three years experience is required although certain education may be substituted. Inspectors operate out of offices located throughout the country.

Safety inspectors examine air personnel for their initial certification and continuing competence; evaluate training programs, equipment and facilities; and evaluate the operations programs of air carriers and other commercial aviation companies.

Other safety inspectors evaluate mechanics and repair facilities for their initial certification and continuing adequacy, evaluate training programs for mechanics, inspect airplanes and related systems for airworthiness, and evaluate the maintenance programs of air carriers and other commercial aviation companies.

Still other safety inspectors inspect prototype or modified aircraft and the production operations of manufacturers. They also issue certificates for all civil aircraft.

Airspace system inspection pilots conduct in-flight inspections of ground-based air navigational facilities to determine if they are operating correctly.

Test pilots check the airworthiness of aircraft by inspecting, flight testing, and evaluating flight performance, engine operation, and the flight characteristics of either prototype airplanes or aircraft that have been modified.

Maintenance mechanics maintain aids to air navigation such as approach light systems serving airport runways, and they also work on the structural, electrical, and mechanical devices which are major parts of other facilities. This may include maintenance and repair of heating, air-conditioning and ventilating systems, electrical generating and power distribution systems, and the buildings and antenna structures which house a wide variety of FAA facilities. These jobs can involve carpentry, painting, plumbing, electrical, and masonry construction and require specialized skills in these areas. Employment may be found in all areas of the country and anywhere that FAA air navigational aids and air traffic control towers or centers are located.

Engineers of all specialties are employed to work on the research and development of all types of new aircraft and of new equipment and devices to increase aviation safety. Some engineers provide guidance in airport design, construction, operation, and maintenance. The following engineering specialists are employed: aerospace, electrical, electronic, mechanical, and civil.

Engineering technicians are also employed to assist engineers by drafting engineering plans, conducting efficiency and performance tests, making calculations, setting up laboratory equipment and instruments, and preparing technical reports, specifications, and estimates.

Physicians are required inasmuch as aviation medicine is a most important field. These physicians study such things as the effects of flying on the human body, the need for oxygen above certain altitudes, effects of fatigue on pilot performance, vision and hearing, the tension and stress factors associated with the air traffic controller's job, and the standards of the various classes of medical examinations required for pilots and other flight crew members.

The FAA also hires *lawyers* to write and interpret Federal Aviation Regulations, and to represent the FAA in legal controversies. *Office staffs* include accountants, public information officers, librarians, photographers, and supporting personnel such as receptionists, secretaries, typists, office machine operators, mail room clerks, and data computer programmers and operators.

In addition to all of the jobs just listed, the FAA operates two federal airports in the Washington, D.C. area (Washington National and Dulles International), where it employs *runway, building,* and *ground maintenance personnel* as well as an *airport administrative staff.*

It should be noted that the Federal Aviation Administration is subject to the same budget and personnel cutbacks as other government agencies. Although some safety experts may claim that the FAA should hire more air traffic controllers and other specialists to handle the ever increasing volume of traffic, it is questionable how much additional money, if any, Congress will appropriate for this purpose in the future. Nevertheless, there will continue to be job opportunities as employees resign, retire, or receive promotions to other positions.

Almost every state has an aeronautics department or commission which may employ some or all of the following: administrative assistants, pilots, field service representatives, accountants and statisticians, stenographers, clerks, typists, engineers and engineering technicians, aeronautical inspectors, safety officers, aircraft mechanics, publications editors, and aviation education officers. Ask your public librarian for the proper name and address of your state aeronautics department so that you can contact it regarding employment opportunities.

FAA AVIATION CAREERS PAMPHLETS

The Federal Aviation Administration has prepared several informative pamphlets on aviation careers which (when this book went to press) were distributed free of charge. Each gives information about training, duties, and job outlook. They may be ordered by writing the Superintendent of Documents, Retail Distribution Division, Consigned Branch, 8610 Cherry Lane, Laurel, MD 20707.

When ordering any of these pamphlets be sure to give the order number as well as the title:

GA-300-122-*Career Pilots and Flight Engineers*
GA-300-123-*Aviation Maintenance*

The flight navigator, like the air traffic controller, must understand and use sohpisticated electronic equipment. Photo: United Airlines.

GA-300-124-*Airport Careers*
GA-300-125-*Aircraft Manufacturing Occupations*
GA-300-126-*Airline Careers*
GA-300-127-*Flight Attendants*
GA-300-128-*Government Careers*

The pamphlet on government careers describes the various career opportunities which exist with the Federal Aviation Administration as well as certain other government agencies.

For information about available openings in the government for jobs in aviation or other fields, write to the Office of Personnel Management, Office of Public Affairs, 1900 E Street, NW, Washington, DC 20415. For further information about the Federal Aviation Administration write to its Public Inquiry Center, Washington, DC 20591.

Passenger airlines are not the only possible source of employment in the air transportation field; air freight carriers employ thousands of pople in many comparable jobs. Photo. United Parcel Service.

CHAPTER 13

YOUR CAREER IN AIR TRANSPORTATION

Aviation is a highly cyclical business which means that it often goes through periods of expansion and retrenchment. During the latter, employees with low seniority can be laid off for an indefinite period of time. Many airlines are unionized and disputes sometimes bring about strikes and layoffs of large numbers of employees. Shift work is necessary in the majority of jobs, and some jobs must be performed under adverse conditions in all kinds of weather. Finally, as can be true in any large company, there is danger of an individual being overlooked for promotion, slotted into a specialized job, and left there. This does not have to happen, however, if you have ability and are not hesitant to speak up for yourself.

Definite advantages offset the limitations. Air transportation is an essential industry which offers a relatively good degree of job security for those who have seniority. Unionized employees tend to enjoy good pay, and on the whole, industry wages are above average. During a recent year the average annual compensation for airline employees was $42,500, including benefits, but do not expect this as a starting salary by any means! Changes and new technical developments in the industry provide constant and exciting career challenges and opportunities for those prepared to take advantage of them. The average airline employee enjoys a certain prestige because flying is still considered glamorous. Fringe benefits are usually generous and unique because they include free and reduced rate transportation, not only on the company's planes, but on most other airlines, too. This can be worth thousands of dollars over an employee's lifetime.

EDUCATION AND PREPARATION:
WHAT TO DO NEXT

If you are really interested in an airline career your best course is to read and learn all you can about the business and discuss with a guidance or career counselor how best to prepare yourself. There are many entry level positions in the airlines which do not call for any further education beyond high school. Other positions call for specialized technical training, some require a college education with emphasis on certain subjects, and a few demand postgraduate degrees.

Whatever the educational requirements of the job you have in mind, you should chart your future as soon as possible to plan how you can achieve your goal. If you do not think you can afford the college education needed, look into the possibility of securing a scholarship or other types of financial assistance, of going to college after work at night, or of obtaining further education while you serve in the armed forces. Any of these avenues may work to get you into the path leading to your career goal.

PREPARING FOR AN AIRLINE CAREER
THROUGH THE ARMED FORCES

The military services offer career opportunities in a range of occupations. Jobs include clerical and administrative work, electrical and electronic occupations and hundreds of other specialties. You can obtain basic and advanced training that will be useful in both military and civilian airline careers.

You may enlist in any one of a variety of programs which involve different combinations of active and reserve duty. Job training available to enlisted individuals depends on the length of their service commitment, their general and technical aptitudes, personal preferences, and the needs of the service at that time.

If the opportunities offered by the military services interest you, look in your telephone book under U.S. Government for the addresses and phone numbers of each service or write to:

USAF Recruiting Service
Randolph Air Force Base,
TX 78150

U.S. Army Recruiting Command
Fort Sheridan, IL 60037

U.S. Coast Guard
Call 800-424-8883 for address of nearest Coast Guard recruiter.
Call 557-0295 if you live in Washington, D.C.

Marine Corps Opportunities
P.O. Box 38901
Los Angeles, CA 90038

Navy Recruiting Command (Code 40)
4015 Wilson Blvd.
Arlington, VA 22208

FINDING YOUR JOB

Airlines occasionally send recruiters to schools and colleges to sign up students before graduation. If you are presently a student, be sure to tell your guidance counselor, faculty adviser, principal, or college personnel officer of your interest in air transportation so you can meet any interviewers who may come to your school or college.

If you live in a large city or town, register with private employment agencies as well as your state employment security office. If you live in a rural area, contact the nearest office of your state employment security service so you can talk with an interviewer and benefit from such advice and help as he or she may give you. This service is free; use it!

If you live near one or more airline offices, visit them and ask about employment opportunities. If you live a great distance from an airport or the office of an airline, write to the personnel departments of airlines listed at the end of this chapter. Tell them of your interests and abilities, and ask how you might apply for a position. Your public librarian may be able to help you obtain a list of fixed base operators in your state should you be interested in starting your career in that end of the business.

THE FUTURE IS YOURS

Although the air transport industry has periods of prosperity and economy, it is here to stay and is certain to continue its growth. Because it offers greater speed and comfort than buses and trains, public use is bound to increase. Furthermore, air freight will increase, as well.

There will be continued demand for technically trained men and women, and for secretaries, typists, computer operators, custodians, ramp service workers, and others. Obviously, the better your education and skills, the greater the rewards to be realized in your career.

Regardless of your position in the industry, your participation in the overall effort will be important, and you can take special pride in your work knowing that you too are making a contribution toward the growth and success of a challenging and exciting industry.

UNITED STATES SCHEDULED AIRLINE MEMBERS OF THE AIR TRANSPORT ASSOCIATION OF AMERICA

Air California
3636 Birch Street
Newport Beach, California
92660

Alaska Airlines
P.O. Box 68900
Seattle-Tacoma
    International Airport
Seattle, Washington 98168

Aloha Airlines
P.O. Box 30028
Honolulu, Hawaii 96820

American Airlines
P.O. Box 61616
Dallas-Fort Worth Airport
Texas 75261

Best Airlines
207 Grandview Drive
Ft. Mitchell, Kentucky 41017

Braniff
P.O. Box 7035
Dallas, Texas 75209

Continental Airlines
333 Clay Street #4040
Houston, Texas 77002

Delta Airlines
Hartsfield Atlanta
    International Airport
Atlanta, Georgia 30320

Eastern Air Lines
Miami International Airport
Miami, Florida 33148

Evergreen International
Airlines
3850 Three Mile Lane
McMinnville, Oregon 97128

Federal Express
Box 727
Memphis, Tennessee 38194

The Flying Tiger Line
P.O. Box 92935
Los Angeles, California 90009

Frontier Airlines
8250 Smith Road
Denver, Colorado 80207

Hawaiian Airlines
P.O. Box 30008
Honolulu International Airport
Honolulu, Hawaii 96820

Jet America Airlines
3521 E. Spring Street
Long Beach, California 90806

Midway Airlines
Midway Airport
5700 South Cicero Avenue
Chicago, Illinois 60638

Muse Air
Muse Air Centre
3535 Travis Street
Dallas, Texas 75204

Northwest Airlines
Minneapolis-St. Paul
  International Airport
St. Paul, Minnesota 55111

Ozark Air Lines
Lambert Field
St. Louis, Missouri 63145

Pan American World Airways
Pan Am Building
New York, New York 10166

Piedmont Airlines
P.O. Box 2720
Winston-Salem,
North Carolina 27156

PSA-Pacific Southwest
  Airlines
3225 North Harbor Drive
San Diego, California 92101

Purolator Courier
131 Morristown Road
Basking Ridge, New Jersey
07920-1652

Republic Airlines
7500 Airline Drive
Minneapolis, Minnesota 55450

Trans World Airlines
605 Third Avenue
New York, New York 10158

United Airlines
P.O. Box 66100
Chicago, Illinois 60666

United Parcel Service
Greenwich Office Park 5
Greeenwich, Connecticut 06830

USAir
Washington National Airport
Washington, D.C. 20001

Western Air Lines
P.O. Box 92005
World Way Postal Center
Los Angeles, California 90009

APPENDIX B

SOURCES OF ADDITIONAL INFORMATION

For names and addresses of supplemental air carriers, intrastate, commuter, and other air services, air taxi and indirect carriers, airports, and in-flight services, see the *World Aviation Directory.*

Airline Employees Association
5600 S. Central Avenue
Chicago, IL 60638
(Reservation, ticket, and
   passenger agents).

Airline Pilots Association
1625 Massachusetts Avenue
   NW
Washington, D.C. 20036

Airport Operators Council
   International Inc.
1700 K Street, NW
Washington, D.C. 20006

Air Transport Association of
   America
1709 New York Avenue, NW
Washington, D.C. 20006

American Association of
   Airport Executives
4224 King Street
Alexandria, VA 22302

Aviation Maintenance Foun-
   dation
Box 2826
Redmond, WA 98073

Flight Engineers' International
   Association
905 16 Street, NW
Washington, D.C. 20006

National Association of Trade
   and Technical Schools
2021 L Street, NW
Washington, D.C. 20036

Public Relations Society of
   America, Inc.
845 Third Avenue
New York, NY 10022

U.S. Federal Aviation
  Administration
Public Inquiry Center
Washington, D.C. 20591

U.S. Office of Personnel
  Management
Office of Public Affairs
1900 E Street, NW
Washington, D.C. 20415

APPENDIX C

BIBLIOGRAPHY OF SUGGESTED READING

Air Transport Association of America; *The People of the Airlines.* Request single copies from Air Transport Association of America, 1709 New York Avenue, N.W., Washington, DC 20006. Enclose a self-addressed, stamped No. 10 envelope.

Air Transport World. Stamford, CN, monthly.

Airport Services Management. Minneapolis, MN, monthly.

Baxter, Neale; *Opportunities in Federal Government Careers.* Lincolnwood, IL: VGM Career Horizons, 1985.

Cadin, Martin; *Boeing 707.* New York, Ballantine Books, 1959.

Conway, McKinley; *The Airport City: Development Concepts for the Twenty-First Century.* Atlanta, GA: Conway Data, 1980.

Foster, Timothy R.; *How to Become an Airline Pilot.* Summit, PA: TAB Books, 1982.

Fruhan, William E., Jr.; *The Fight for Competitive Advantage: A Study of the United States Domestic Carriers.* Boston: Harvard Business School Press, 1982.

Garrison, Paul; *How the Air Traffic Control System Works.* Summit, PA: TAB Books, 1979.

Greif, Martin; *The Airport Book: From Landing Field to Modern Terminal.* Atlanta, GA: Susan Hunter Publishing, 1979.

Griffin, Jeff W.; *How to Become a Flight Engineer.* Summit, PA: TAB Books, 1982.

Kelly, Charles J., Jr.; *Sky's the Limit: The History of the Airlines.* Salem, NH: Ayer Co. Publishers, Inc., 1971.

Lowery, John; *The Professional Pilot.* Ames, IA: Iowa State University Press, 1983.

Martin, Paul K., Editor; *Airline Handbook.* Cranston, RI: Aero Travel Research, 1985.

O'Connor, William E.; *An Introduction to Airline Economics.* New York: Praeger Publishing, 1985.

Paradis, Adrian A.; *Opportunities in Transportation Careers.* Lincolnwood, IL: VGM Career Horizons, 1983.

Rich, Elizabeth; *What It's Like to Be a Flight Attendant.* Briarcliff Manor, NY: Stein and Day, 1981.

Rodney, Morgan R.; *Flight Facts for Private Pilots.* Fallbrook, CA: Aero Publications; Inc., 1983.

Serling, Robert J.; *Eagle: The Story of American Airlines.* New York: St. Martins Press, 1985.

_____, *The Only Way to Fly.* Garden City, NY: Doubleday, 1976.

Shives, Bob, and Thompson, Bill; *Airlines of North America.* Sarasota, FL: Crestline Publishing Co., 1984.

Smith, Myron J.; *Commercial Aviation: An Annotated Bibliography.* West Cornwall, CT: Locust Hill Press, 1986.

Smith, Peter; *Air Freight.* Salem, NH: Faber and Faber, 1974.

Solberg, Carl; *Conquest of the Skies, a History of Commercial Aviation in America.* Boston: Little, Brown & Co., 1979.

Stilley, Frank; *Here Is Your Career, Airline Pilot.* New York: G.P. Putnam's Sons, 1978.

Taneja, Nawal K.; *Airlines in Transition.* Lexington, MA: Lexington Books, 1981.

_____ *The Commercial Airlines Industry: Managerial Practices and Policies.* Lexington, MA: Lexington Books, 1976.

World Aviation Directory. Washington, DC: Ziff-Davis Publishing Company.

Wyckoff, D. Daryl, and Maister, David H.; *The Domestic Airline Industry.* Lexington, MA: Lexington Books, 1977.

VGM CAREER BOOKS

OPPORTUNITIES IN

Available in both paperback and hardbound editions

Accounting Careers
Acting Careers
Advertising Careers
Agriculture Careers
Airline Careers
Animal and Pet Care
Appraising Valuation Science
Architecture
Automotive Service
Banking
Beauty Culture
Biological Sciences
Book Publishing Careers
Broadcasting Careers
Building Construction Trades
Business Communication Careers
Business Management
Cable Television
Carpentry Careers
Chemical Engineering
Chemistry Careers
Child Care Careers
Chiropractic Health Care
Civil Engineering Careers
Commercial Art and Graphic
  Design
Computer Aided Design
  and Computer Aided Mfg
Computer Science Careers
Counseling & Development
Crafts Careers
Dance
Data Processing Careers
Dental Care
Drafting Careers
Electrical Trades
Electronic and Electrical
  Engineering
Energy Careers
Engineering Technology Careers
Environmental Careers
Fashion Careers
Federal Government Careers
Film Careers
Financial Careers
Fire Protection Services
Fitness Careers
Food Services
Foreign Language Careers
Forestry Careers
Gerontology Careers
Government Service
Graphic Communications
Health and
  Medical Careers

High Tech Careers
Home Economics Careers
Hospital Administration
Hotel & Motel Management
Industrial Design
Insurance Careers
Interior Design
Journalism Careers
Landscape Architecture
Law Careers
Law Enforcement and
  Criminal Justice
Library and Information
  Science
Machine Trades
Magazine Publishing Careers
Management
Marine & Maritime Careers
Marketing Careers
Materials Science
Mechanical Engineering
Microelectronics
Modeling Careers
Music Careers
Nursing Careers
Nutrition Careers
Occupational Therapy
  Careers
Office Occupations
Opticianry
Optometry
Packaging Science
Paralegal Careers
Paramedical Careers
Part-time & Summer Jobs
Personnel Management
Pharmacy Careers
Photography
Physical Therapy Careers
Podiatric Medicine
Printing Careers
Psychiatry
Psychology
Public Relations Careers
Real Estate
Recreation and Leisure
Refrigeration and
  Air Conditioning
Religious Service
Robotics Careers
Sales & Marketing
Secretarial Careers
Securities Industry
Speech-Language Pathology
  Careers
Sports & Athletics
Sports Medicine
State and Local Government
Teaching Careers

Technical Communications
Telecommunications
Theatrical Design
  & Production
Transportation Careers
Travel Careers
Veterinary Medicine Careers
Vocational and Technical
  Careers
Word Processing
Writing Careers
Your Own Service Business

WOMEN IN

Communications
Engineering
Finance
Government
Management
Science
Their Own Business

CAREERS IN

Accounting
Business
Communications
Computers
Health Care
Science

CAREER DIRECTORIES

Careers Encyclopedia
Occupational Outlook Handbook

CAREER PLANNING

How to Get People to Do
  Things Your Way
How to Have a Winning
  Job Interview
How to Land a Better Job
How to Write a Winning
  Résumé
Life Plan
Planning Your Career Change
Planning Your Career of
  Tomorrow
Planning Your College
  Education
Planning Your Military Career
Planning Your Own Home
  Business
Planning Your Young Child's
  Education

SURVIVAL GUIDES

High School Survival Guide
College Survival Guide

 VGM Career Horizons
A Division of National Textbook Company
4255 West Touhy Avenue
Lincolnwood, Illinois 60646-1975 U.S.A.

11.95